Communication in Instruction

Communication in Instruction: Beyond Traditional Classroom Settings explores the various challenges we face when trying to teach others in various contexts beyond traditional classroom settings, as well as the possible strategies for overcoming them.

Instructional communication is a research field that focuses on the role communication plays in instructing others. Although many resources focus on effective instructional communication strategies within a traditional classroom setting, this book expands the scope to include diverse settings where instructional communication also occurs (e.g., risk and crisis situations, health care contexts, business settings), as well as new directions where instructional communication research and practice are (or ought to be) headed.

Whether we are trying to teach a youngster to ride a bike, to help a friend evaluate the claims made on an advertisement, or to conduct a safety drill with colleagues in the workplace, we are engaging in instructional communication. If we want to do so effectively, however, we need to equip ourselves with best practice tools and strategies for doing so. That is what this book is intended to do. In it, you will read about how to teach advocacy to health care practitioners, guide others to become socialised in a new workplace setting, employ strategies for teaching digital media literacy to nondigital natives, and use Artificial Intelligence (AI) and robots when instructing and engaging strategies for instruction around socially relevant issues such as religion, politics, and violence. Together, they point to some of the ways instructional communication scholarship may be used to explore and inform best practices across communication contexts.

The chapters in this book were originally published in *Communication Education*.

Deanna D. Sellnow and **Timothy L. Sellnow** are Professors of Strategic Communication in the Nicholson School of Communication and Media at the University of Central Florida. Collectively, their research focuses on health, risk, crisis, instructional communication, and the intersection among them. They have published numerous books and articles in regional, national, and international journals, as well as conducted and presented research in myriad countries around the world.

Communication in Instruction
Beyond Traditional Classroom Settings

Edited by
Deanna D. Sellnow and Timothy L. Sellnow

LONDON AND NEW YORK

First published 2021
by Routledge
2 Park Square, Milton Park, Abingdon, Oxon OX14 4RN

and by Routledge
605 Third Avenue, New York, NY 10158

Routledge is an imprint of the Taylor & Francis Group, an informa business

© 2021 National Communication Association

All rights reserved. No part of this book may be reprinted or reproduced or utilised in any form or by any electronic, mechanical, or other means, now known or hereafter invented, including photocopying and recording, or in any information storage or retrieval system, without permission in writing from the publishers.

Trademark notice: Product or corporate names may be trademarks or registered trademarks, and are used only for identification and explanation without intent to infringe.

British Library Cataloguing in Publication Data
A catalogue record for this book is available from the British Library

ISBN13: 978-0-367-48126-1 (hbk)
ISBN13: 978-0-367-77633-6 (pbk)
ISBN13: 978-1-003-03813-9 (ebk)

Typeset in Minion Pro
by Newgen Publishing UK

Publisher's Note
The publisher accepts responsibility for any inconsistencies that may have arisen during the conversion of this book from journal articles to book chapters, namely the inclusion of journal terminology.

Disclaimer
Every effort has been made to contact copyright holders for their permission to reprint material in this book. The publishers would be grateful to hear from any copyright holder who is not here acknowledged and will undertake to rectify any errors or omissions in future editions of this book.

Contents

Citation Information vii
Notes on Contributors ix

Introduction: communication and instruction beyond the traditional classroom 1
Deanna D. Sellnow and Timothy L. Sellnow

1 Spewing nonsense [or not]: communication competence and socialization in optics and photonics workplaces 6
Kelly Norris Martin, Amy L. Housley Gaffney, Anne E. Leak, Jes Nelson, Alexandria T. Cervantes, Katherine Louise Gardener, Brandon L. Clark and Benjamin M. Zwickl

2 Teaching advocacy communication to pediatric residents: the efficacy of applied improvisational theater (AIT) as an instructional tool 30
Krista Hoffmann-Longtin, Jason M. Organ, Jill V. Helphinstine, Deanna R. Reinoso, Zachary S. Morgan and Elizabeth Weinstein

3 Fake news, phishing, and fraud: a call for research on digital media literacy education beyond the classroom 52
Nicole M. Lee

4 A new research agenda: instructional practices of activists mobilizing for science 59
Meghnaa Tallapragada

5 I, teacher: using artificial intelligence (AI) and social robots in communication and instruction 65
Chad Edwards, Autumn Edwards, Patric R. Spence and Xialing Lin

6 Bridging campus and community: religion and violence as expansive and socially relevant communication research 73
Sean M. Horan and Courtney N. Wright

7 Health communication as an instructional communication context beyond the classroom 80
Teresa L. Thompson

8 Response to special issue on communication and instruction beyond the traditional classroom 83
Matthew W. Seeger

9 A call for a pedagogy of empathy 87
Carolyn Calloway-Thomas

10 Riddles, mysteries, and enigmas: communication, teaching, and learning beyond the traditional classroom 92
Deanna P. Dannels

Index 94

Citation Information

The chapters in this book were originally published in *Communication Education* volume 67, issue 4 (October 2018). When citing this material, please use the original page numbering for each article, as follows:

Introduction
Introduction to this special issue on communication and instruction beyond the traditional classroom
Deanna D. Sellnow and Timothy L. Sellnow
Communication Education volume 67, issue 4 (October 2018), pp. 409–413

Chapter 1
Spewing nonsense [or not]: communication competence and socialization in optics and photonics workplaces
Kelly Norris Martin, Amy L. Housley Gaffney, Anne E. Leak, Jes Nelson, Alexandria T. Cervantes, Katherine Louise Gardener, Brandon L. Clark and Benjamin M. Zwickl
Communication Education volume 67, issue 4 (October 2018), pp. 414–437

Chapter 2
Teaching advocacy communication to pediatric residents: the efficacy of applied improvisational theater (AIT) as an instructional tool
Krista Hoffmann-Longtin, Jason M. Organ, Jill V. Helphinstine, Deanna R. Reinoso, Zachary S. Morgan and Elizabeth Weinstein
Communication Education volume 67, issue 4 (October 2018), pp. 438–459

Chapter 3
Fake news, phishing, and fraud: a call for research on digital media literacy education beyond the classroom
Nicole M. Lee
Communication Education volume 67, issue 4 (October 2018), pp. 460–466

Chapter 4
A new research agenda: instructional practices of activists mobilizing for science
Meghnaa Tallapragada
Communication Education volume 67, issue 4 (October 2018), pp. 467–472

Chapter 5
I, teacher: using artificial intelligence (AI) and social robots in communication and instruction
Chad Edwards, Autumn Edwards, Patric R. Spence and Xialing Lin
Communication Education volume 67, issue 4 (October 2018), pp. 473–480

Chapter 6
Bridging campus and community: religion and violence as expansive and socially relevant communication research
Sean M. Horan and Courtney N. Wright
Communication Education volume 67, issue 4 (October 2018), pp. 481–487

Chapter 7
Health communication as an instructional communication context beyond the classroom
Teresa L. Thompson
Communication Education volume 67, issue 4 (October 2018), pp. 488–490

Chapter 8
Response to special issue on communication and instruction beyond the traditional classroom
Matthew W. Seeger
Communication Education volume 67, issue 4 (October 2018), pp. 491–494

Chapter 9
A call for a pedagogy of empathy
Carolyn Calloway-Thomas
Communication Education volume 67, issue 4 (October 2018), pp. 495–499

Chapter 10
Riddles, mysteries, and enigmas: communication, teaching, and learning beyond the traditional classroom
Deanna P. Dannels
Communication Education volume 67, issue 4 (October 2018), pp. 500–501

For any permission-related enquiries please visit:
www.tandfonline.com/page/help/permissions

Notes on Contributors

Carolyn Calloway-Thomas, World Communication Association, Indiana University, Bloomington, USA; African American and African Diaspora Studies, Indiana University, Bloomington, USA.

Alexandria T. Cervantes, Department of Mathematics and Statistics, California State University Monterey Bay, Seaside, CA, USA.

Brandon L. Clark, Department of Mathematics, West Virginia University, Morgantown, WV, USA.

Deanna P. Dannels, Department of Communication, North Carolina State University, Raleigh, NC, USA.

Autumn Edwards, School of Communication, Western Michigan University, Kalamazoo, USA.

Chad Edwards, School of Communication, Western Michigan University, Kalamazoo, USA.

Jill V. Helphinstine, Department of Pediatrics, Indiana University School of Medicine, Indianapolis, IN, USA.

Krista Hoffmann-Longtin, Department of Communication Studies, Indiana University Purdue University Indianapolis, Indianapolis, IN, USA.

Sean M. Horan, Department of Communication, Fairfield University, Fairfield, CT, USA.

Amy L. Housley Gaffney, Oral Communication Center, Hamilton College, Clinton, NY, USA.

Anne E. Leak, School of Physics and Astronomy, Rochester Institute of Technology, Rochester, NY, USA.

Nicole M. Lee, Department of Communication, North Carolina State University, Raleigh, NC, USA.

Xialing Lin, Department of Corporate Communication, Penn State University-Worthington Scranton, Dunmore, USA.

Katherine Louise Gardener, School of Communication, Rochester Institute of Technology, Rochester, NY, USA.

Kelly Norris Martin, School of Communication, Rochester Institute of Technology, Rochester, NY, USA.

Zachary S. Morgan, Office of the Provost, California Institute of the Arts, Valencia, CA, USA.

Jes Nelson, School of Communication, Rochester Institute of Technology, Rochester, NY, USA.

Jason M. Organ, Department of Anatomy and Cell Biology, Indiana University School of Medicine, Indianapolis, IN, USA.

Deanna R. Reinoso, Department of Pediatrics, Indiana University School of Medicine, Indianapolis, IN, USA.

Matthew W. Seeger, Department of Communication, Wayne State University, Detroit, MI, USA.

Deanna Sellnow, Nicholson School of Communication and Media, University of Central Florida, Orlando, USA.

Timothy Sellnow, Nicholson School of Communication and Media, University of Central Florida, Orlando, USA.

Patric R. Spence, Nicholson School of Communication and Media, University of Central Florida, Orlando, USA.

Meghnaa Tallapragada, Department of Communication, College of Behavioral, Social and Health Sciences, Clemson University, Clemson, USA.

Teresa L. Thompson, Department of Communication, University of Dayton, Dayton, USA.

Elizabeth Weinstein, Departments of Emergency Medicine and Pediatrics, Indiana University School of Medicine, Indianapolis, IN, USA.

Courtney N. Wright, College of Communication and Information, University of Tennessee-Knoxville, Knoxville, TN, USA.

Benjamin M. Zwickl, School of Physics and Astronomy, Rochester Institute of Technology, Rochester, NY, USA.

INTRODUCTION

Communication and instruction beyond the traditional classroom

Deanna D. Sellnow and Timothy L. Sellnow

Most people are familiar with the Chinese proverb, "Give a man [sic] a fish and you feed him for a day. Teach a man to fish and you feed him for a lifetime" (Tripp, 1970, p. 76). Those of us studying instructional communication not only concur, but also argue that effective communication is critical to successful teaching and learning in all contexts. Moreover, we assert that many communication initiatives, interventions, and campaigns are destined to fail when the messages do not instruct receivers about how and why to act on the information.

The term *instructional communication* was originally conceived in the 1970s as a means to distinguish it from *communication education*, which was broadly defined as instruction in communication (how to teach interpersonal communication, group communication, public communication, etc.). Instructional communication, on the other hand, referred to the role of communication *in* instruction (Richmond & Frymier, 2010). Scholars believed that conceptualizing instructional communication in this broader context would encourage a wealth of instructional research occurring in a variety of communication contexts (e.g., health, intercultural, interpersonal, family, organizational, political). In fact, Mottet and Beebe (2006) poignantly confirmed that instructional communication research "is not limited to the traditional primary, secondary, and higher education classroom, but can also be applied to non-traditional instructional settings" (p. 5).

Unfortunately, however, our observations over several decades indicate that this did not happen; at least not overtly. Instead, scholars studying the role of communication in instruction in various subfields often coined their own terms. For example, health communication scholars created the term *health interventions,* organizational communication scholars referred to such instructional research as *professional training and development,* and public relations scholars adopted the term *communication campaigns.* Although we cannot be certain as to why scholars in various communication subfields conceived unique terms to define what is essentially instructional communication research, one possible explanation is that we (instructional communication scholars) have not articulated what we mean by instructional communication as clearly as we could. Another is that we have not highlighted the intersections among our shared research goals, methods, and outcome measures as explicitly as we should. What is clear, however, is that the call to expand the scope of instructional communication research beyond traditional classroom contexts has not materialized to the degree instructional communication researchers had hoped it would when they first conceived it as distinct from communication education.

Our goal in this special issue is to renew the call for overtly advancing instructional communication scholarship as it occurs across communication contexts. In renewing this call for examining the role of instructional communication across contexts, we join forces with a number of colleagues that are also committed to this cause (e.g., Chory & Horan, 2018; Donovan, Love, Mackert, Vangelisti, & Ring, 2017; Horan & Afifi, 2014; Sellnow et al., 2015; Sellnow & Sellnow, in press; Waldeck & LaBelle, 2016; Sprague, 2002; Valenzano & Wallace, 2017). We hope that by calling attention to the expansive scope of the instructional communication research agenda in this special issue, we will crystalize the role of instructional communication across contexts in ways that entice more scholars to join us in studying the role of communication in instruction beyond traditional classroom settings.

We ground our rationale in a larger argument about the current state of the communication discipline. To clarify, although defining theories and research based on communication contexts served us well when communication was a relatively new discipline seeking to establish ourselves firmly in the academy, continuing to do so may do us more harm than good. That is, we have become unnecessarily fragmented in the silos we have built based on context. We believe the time has come to employ communication theories and methods based on research goals and desired outcomes regardless of context. It seems, for example, that communication scholars study interpersonal communication across contexts and persuasive communication across contexts, among others. We believe, just as many communication subfields are not context dependent, neither should instructional communication be. To clarify, if one's goal is to examine the role of communication in achieving desired learning outcomes in the workplace, that is instructional communication in an organizational context. If one examines the degree to which doctors' instructions about postoperative care are followed by patients, that is instructional communication in a healthcare context. If one seeks to develop a warning message that encourages people to take appropriate actions to avoid the perils of a natural disaster, that is instructional communication in a risk and crisis communication context. Thus, the following articles are grounded in the spirit of this stance for moving the field of communication both together and forward (in this case, focused on instructional communication research in particular) in the years to come.

This special issue consists of two research articles, four agenda-setting pieces, and three expert responses designed to encourage readers to think outside the box of instructional communication only as it occurs in traditional classrooms. The first research article, "Teaching advocacy communication to pediatric residents: the efficacy of applied improvisation as a training tool," by Krista Hoffmann-Longtin and colleagues explores the utility of using applied improvisational theater as an instructional method for teaching pediatric residents how to communicate effectively with worried and confused patients and their families. In learning these important skills, healthcare practitioners have the potential to reclaim themselves as trusted experts that can help clients make meaning of health information they receive from the Internet and other information sources. The article clearly demonstrates the value of examining instructional practices as they influence learning in a health communication context.

The second research article, "Spewing nonsense [or not]: communication competence and socialization in optics and photonics workplaces," by Kelly Norris Martin and colleagues, examines how professionals in the optics and photonics industry are socialized to enact the norms of effective communication in their workplaces. Through a qualitative analysis of 33 interviews with employees from 15 different optics and photonics companies, they revealed five primary themes regarding effective communication norms and expectations: proactive questioning, efficient decision making, familial-like humor, tactful translation, and fluent modality switching. Ultimately, they argue that communication competence requires cross-occupational communication that can be taught via systematic and intentional communication in the disciplines instruction. As such, this article makes a valuable contribution to our understanding of instructional communication in an organizational communication context.

The first of the agenda-setting manuscripts, "Fake news, phishing, and fraud: a call for research on digital media literacy education outside the classroom," by Nicole Lee and Will Ryan points to recent and growing trends to spread false online news and fraud. They respond to this extensive distortion and deception with a call for teaching digital media literacy to adults generally and to older adults specifically to teach them the skills required to evaluate the information and sources they discover online, manage private personal information when participating in social media environments, and avoid falling victim to cybercrimes targeting them. They rightly point out that most digital media literacy instruction targets children, adolescents, and college students; however, more instructional training and research ought to focus on programs tailored to nondigital natives. This need is particularly pressing given that polls conducted as recently as 2016 indicate that more cybercrimes are committed against people 60 years old and older than any other age group (FBI, 2017). They propose several avenues to fill these gaps in instructional research and teaching about digital media literacy beyond traditional classroom walls. Doing so would make an important contribution to the scholarly conversation about communication in digital media literacy instruction.

In her article, "A new research agenda: instructional practices of activists mobilizing for science," Meghnaa Tallapragada proposes a related research agenda to address the growing concern over fake news and alternative facts that attempt to debunk the credibility of science. At the core of her agenda, Tallapragada contends that instructional communication and research can help science advocates make science knowledge accessible to diverse publics and to policy makers and, in doing so, refute false information with evidence-based scientific facts. For example, research could explore how scientists explain science to nonscientists and both groups could work together to cocreate shared understanding. Research could also examine the degree to which mobilization influences not only science literacy but also attitudes toward science, as well as the effects of various compliance-gaining strategies used by activists to mobilize others to join the cause. Ultimately, her article makes a strong case for instructional communication and research in science communication contexts.

In their article, "I, teacher: using artificial intelligence (AI) and social robots in communication and instruction," Chad Edwards, Autumn Edwards, and Patric Spence focus on the compelling need for more research deconstructing the pros and cons of using AI and social robots, as well as how they might be used collaboratively to enhance teaching and learning practices of instructors rather than replace them.

In essence, they argue that human–machine communication (HMC) has found its way into educational contexts, both within and beyond traditional classroom walls, and its use is likely to grow. Thus, they confirm arguments made by Kaufmann and Tatum (2017) that the time is ripe for replicative instructional research that explores how a variety of human-to-human constructs such as teacher immediacy, credibility, clarity, and humor play out when the instructional interactions take place instead between humans and machines. They aptly conclude that the need for research examining HMC in instructional contexts both within and beyond traditional classrooms will continue to grow. The time to begin that scholarly exchange is now. Instructional research has much to contribute to the relatively new context of human–machine communication.

Sean Horan and Courtney Wright call for expanding instructional research to explore its role in shedding new light on socially relevant issues in their article, "Bridging campus and community: religion and violence as expansive and socially relevant communication research." The two specific areas they focus on are the role of communication and instruction in mitigating socially relevant issues surrounding religion and violence. Essentially, they advise instructional communication scholars to tackle these issues by exploring how external factors, diverse identities, and relational dynamics influence communication, teaching, and learning around religion and violence. They contend that it is both our responsibility and obligation to do so, in part, because by not doing so we make room for pseudocommunication experts to offer misguided instruction and training. Communication scholars must be the go-to sources for evidence-based teaching and learning not only in the academy but in the communities within which we live. Ultimately, their article makes a strong case for extending the boundaries of instructional research to explore the publics' understanding of and related actions taken in response to socially relevant issues occurring in religious communication contexts, as well as on those focused on violence.

Finally, we include forward-thinking responses from three experts with primary research foci in intercultural (Carolyn Calloway-Thomas), risk and crisis (Matthew Seeger), and health (Theresa Thompson). Each of them considers the articles presented here, as well as their own research agendas in ways that suggest future avenues for research in instructional communication beyond traditional classrooms walls. We intentionally selected respondents that do not consider instructional communication to be part of their primary personal research agenda or necessarily even a focus within their primary communication research subfields. Our reasons for doing so are twofold. First, we hope their comments will help illuminate what scholars in other communication subfields perceive instructional communication and research to be. As such, their comments may point to additional research and dialogue we ought to engage in to help our communication colleagues understand instructional communication as we intend it. Second, we hope they will bring ideas for future instructional communication research situated in their subfields back to their colleagues and, in doing so, contribute to achieving our goal of expanding the scope of instructional communication research beyond traditional classroom contexts.

In sum, we hope that these articles taken together spur the thinking of our readers regarding ways they might integrate instructional communication research into their future work. As such, we hope to engage in fruitful scholarly discussions about the role and value of instructional research in a variety of contexts both within and beyond traditional classroom walls. Such a renewed dedication to instructional communication research in all contexts has the potential to address important communication challenges in an ever-evolving world where the communication landscape is continuously shifting.

References

Chory, R. M., & Horan, S. M. (2018). [Re]Negotiating power and influence in the classroom. In M. L. Houser & A. M. Hosek (Eds.), *Handbook of instructional communication: Rhetorical and relational perspectives* (pp. 112–125). New York, NY: Routledge.

Donovan, E., Love, B., Mackert, M., Vangelisti, A., & Ring, D. (2017). Health communication: A future direction for instructional communication research. *Communication Education, 66*(4), 490–492.

Federal Bureau of Investigation/Internet Crime Complaint Center. (2017). *2016 internet crime report*. Washington, DC: Author.

Horan, S. M., & Afifi, T. D. (2014). Advancing instructional communication: Integrating a biosocial approach. *Communication Education, 63*, 383–404.

Kaufmann, R., & Tatum, N. T. (2017). Do we know what we think we know? On the importance of replication in instructional communication research. *Communication Education, 66*(4), 479–481.

Mottet, T. P., & Beebe, S. A. (2006). Foundations of instructional communication. In T. P. Motet, V. P. Richmond, & J. C. McCroskey's (Eds.), *Handbook of instructional communication: Rhetorical and relational perspectives* (pp. 3–32). Boston, MA: Allyn & Bacon.

Richmond, V. P., & Frymier, A. B. (2010). Communication education and instructional development. In J. W. Chesebro (Ed.), *A century of transformation: Studies in honor of the 100th anniversary of the eastern communication association* (pp. 310–328). New York, NY: Oxford.

Sellnow, D. D., Limperos, A., Frisby, B. N., Sellnow, T. L., Spence, P. R., & Downs, E. (2015). Expanding the scope of instructional communication research: Looking beyond classroom contexts. *Communication Studies, 66*, 417–432.

Sellnow, D. D., & Sellnow, T. L. (in press). The IDEA model for effective instructional risk and crisis communication by emergency managers and other key spokespersons. *Journal of Emergency Management*.

Sprague, J. (2002). *Communication education*: The spiral continues. *Communication Education, 51*, 337–354.

Tripp, R. T. (Ed.). (1970). *The international thesaurus of quotations*. New York, NY: Ty Crowell Company.

Valenzano, III, J. M., & Wallace, S. P. (2017). Expanding and exporting instructional communication scholarship: A necessary new direction. *Communication Education, 66*(4), 483–484.

Waldeck, J. H., & LaBelle, S. (2016). Theoretical and methodological approaches to instructional communication. In P. L. Witt (Ed.), *Communication and learning* (pp. 67–101). Berlin: DeGruyter Mouton.

Spewing nonsense [or not]: communication competence and socialization in optics and photonics workplaces

Kelly Norris Martin, Amy L. Housley Gaffney, Anne E. Leak, Jes Nelson, Alexandria T. Cervantes, Katherine Louise Gardener, Brandon L. Clark and Benjamin M. Zwickl

ABSTRACT
This study investigated how managers, entry-level employees, and hiring professionals in the optics and photonics industry socialize each other to enact the communication norms and expectations in their workplaces. A qualitative analysis of transcripts from interviews conducted with 33 employees at 15 companies produced five prevalent themes related to what optics and photonics employees consider competent communication (proactive questioning, efficient decision-making, familial-like humor, tactful translation, and fluent modality switching) and three socialization processes (presumed competence, informal mentoring, and structured training). These competencies and processes necessitate what we term *cross-occupational communication*: an interactive, iterative process involving communicative needs assessment, information exchange, and rhetorical/situational flexibility with groups distinct in background, training, and occupational role. It is difficult to create workplace-like experiences that truly capture the field-specific communication practices involved in organizational socialization within traditional classrooms; therefore, we argue for systematic and intentional communication in the disciplines instruction that considers cross-occupational communication needs in the workforce.

So a lot of the times I end up talking with sales people, but then other times I'm just talking to the customer directly. Sometimes customers or sales associates are technical people and understand the nitty gritty, but sometimes they're more like systems level people, and so they understand enough to pick out the projector and the screen, but they don't necessarily know how to do lens design. There's a lot of different levels of technical understanding. It's about trying to figure out how to communicate with people, and not dumb it down so much that it doesn't mean anything, but also not overwhelm them by spewing nonsense at them.—entry-level employee

Students don't go to conferences, and I take those very seriously. So when you [new employees] do a presentation at a conference, I'm not going to let them just throw it together and go to the conference. That's a multiweek effort, first, they give me their junk and then we're going to improve on it. ... That's how you teach them to be able to do a presentation ... that is of very high caliber.—manager

These two quotations—one from an entry-level employee at an optics company and the other from a Principal Investigator at an academic research lab—suggest that, contrary to some research, employees can move beyond the flawed assumption that effective communication is a simple formula based on a list of tips (Kedrowicz & Taylor, 2013; Martin & Gaffney, 2016). Instead, employees here recognized both the complexity and high-level stakes of communicating technical and complex information to nonscientific audiences. More specifically, they articulated that—at both the managerial and entry levels—effective communication necessitates tailoring instructional messages to the rhetorical situation. Moreover, these comments suggest that employees in the optics and photonics industry saw teaching (whether informally or formally) new hires how to be competent communicators to be part of their roles and responsibilities.

Research focused on communication and instruction in STEM disciplines is critically important as employers do expect employees to be effective communicators. In fact, recent studies indicate that communication plays a central role in the ability to become an influential member of the scientific community (National Academies of Sciences, Engineering, and Medicine, 2018). An MIT alumni study, for instance, found that communication is a necessary skill for innovation and leadership (Wang, 2015). The desire to employ people with strong communication skills is not a new phenomenon, either (Carnevale, Smith, & Melton, 2011; Committee on Prospering in the Global Economy of the 21st Century, 2007; Fabris, 2015; Tryggvason, Thouless, Dutta, Ceccio, & Tilbury, 2001). In the National Academies report on "Developing Transferable Knowledge and Skills in the 21st Century," Pellegrino and Hilton (2012) reviewed 59 international papers on 21st century skills sought by employers and discovered communication to be one of the four most frequently mentioned. What these studies often fail to explain, however, is what employers mean by effective communication. Furthermore, perspectives of managers at large companies dominate the conversation over those at small and midsized organizations, and in-depth qualitative research based on data gathered directly from within STEM industries is sparse.

Communication in the Disciplines (CID) research attempts to address these gaps but most of it occurs in academic classroom and laboratory settings. Even though CID research stresses the importance of conducting field-specific needs assessments, very little CID research draws on programmatic explorations of communication situated in the actual workplace environment. In this study, we extend the scope of CID research by looking at communication within a previously unexamined field—optics and photonics—from the perspectives of managers, entry-level employees, and hiring officials. In particular, we examine the ways in which employees socialize each other to enact the norms of effective communication in their organizations. Thus, this study makes important theoretical and practical contributions to both organizational socialization and CID research and practice regarding how to teach field-specific communication skills within and beyond the classroom.

Organizational socialization

Organizational socialization theories suggest that people are socialized into norms and practices of an organization through a variety of formal and informal processes

(Antonacopoulou & Güttel, 2010; Batistič & Kaše, 2015; Bauer, Bodner, Erdogan, Truxillo, & Tucker, 2007; Commeiras, Loubes, & Bories-Azeau, 2013; Kowtha, 2018; Saks & Gruman, 2018; Saks, Uggerslev, & Fassina, 2007). Although definitions of organizational socialization vary, most describe it as "introductory events and activities by which individuals come to know and make sense out of their newfound work experiences" (Katz, 1980, p. 88). The assumption is that each organization is characterized by unique cultural characteristics that include specialized knowledge, formal standards of conduct, service orientations, social status, professional identity, and education and training (Kedrowicz, Fish, & Hammond, 2015).

Organizational socialization research identifies a variety of strategies used to socialize newcomers. For example, Van Maanen and Schein (1979) propose newcomers use six main tactics: collective–individual, formal–informal, investiture–divestiture, serial–disjunctive, sequential–random and fixed–variable. Jones (1986, p. 263) condenses these tactics into three groups organized on a continuum according to functions: context, content, and social aspects. Contextual tactics (collective–individual, formal–informal) explain job-specific skills and information (e.g., company practices, norms, and expectations). Social tactics (investiture–divestiture, serial–disjunctive) introduce new employees to their roles through mentoring from senior colleagues or by observing role models. Content tactics (fixed–variable, sequential–random) provide a timeline about when newcomers are likely to be accepted (e.g., probationary employment periods). These timelines afford new employees a means by which to monitor their own progress. Overall, these "institutionalized" tactics socialize entry-level employees into the organizational culture (Jones, 1986; Saks et al., 2007). Moreover, social and content tactics are the most important predictors of newcomer adjustment (Bauer et al., 2007), and social tactics may be the most important "because they provide the social cues and facilitation necessary during learning processes" (Jones, 1986, p. 266).

Tactics aside, the degree to which someone fits within a company's culture depends largely on their apparent enthusiasm for the organization and their responsibilities in it. Schaufeli, Salanova, Gonzalez-Roma, and Bakker (2002), for example, discovered that "work engagement," defined as "a positive, fulfilling, work-related state of mind that is characterized by vigor, dedication and absorption" (p. 74), is critical to successful socialization. Other studies reveal that newcomer proactive behaviors such as seeking feedback have a positive impact on work engagement. In essence, when companies make a concerted effort to socialize newcomers, new employees feel inspired to perform well and display increased energy for, dedication to, and focus on work (Saks & Gruman, 2018; Schaufeli & Bakker, 2010).[1]

CID

In academic communities, research confirms that students learn to communicate in disciplinary ways; that is, they are socialized into particular disciplinary ways of communicating. CID pedagogy argues that communication skills are best taught and learned when tied to discipline-specific situations (Dannels, 2001) such as engineering (Bousaba et al., 2014; Canary et al., 2014; Dannels, 2002, 2003; Dannels, Anson, Bullard, & Peretti, 2003; Darling, 2005; Darling & Dannels, 2003), business (Cyphert, 2002; Lucas, 2016), design (Dannels, 2005; Dannels & Martin, 2008; Dannels, Gaffney, & Martin, 2008; Morton &

O'Brien, 2005; Nathans-Kelly & Evans, 2017), and healthcare (Brasseur, 2012; Haber & Lingard, 2001; Hyvärinen, Isotalus, Katajavuori, & Tanskanen, 2010, 2012; Kedrowicz, 2015; Lingard & Haber, 1999; Lingard, Garwood, Schryer, & Spafford, 2003; Vrchota, 2011). Preprofessional and STEM programs have received the majority of attention in CID research, in part because of the unique scientific knowledge and technical expertise required in them. This distinct disciplinary knowledge must be understood in order to provide appropriate communication recommendations for success.

Although the CID framework stresses field-specific preparation, minimal investigations have been conducted within professional environments. This may be due, in part, to the challenges imposed when gathering data in organizations where time is treated as billable, time spent away from paid tasks (e.g., to participate in interviews) must be approved by higher-ups, employees are often suspicious of researchers, and scheduling interviews is logistically difficult. As Vrchota (2011) notes, "Since the motivation for including communication experiences in coursework is often for the purpose of professional preparation, the lack of scholarly activity in this area represents a significant void in CXC [Communication Across the Curriculum] research" (p. 212).

Even when CID studies focus specifically on data collected directly from the professional world, evidence is based primarily on surveys distributed to industry professionals that have temporarily entered an educational setting as a guest, or from instructors who have entered the academic setting after working in industry. One exception is in the healthcare industry. Professional healthcare educators often conduct instructional sessions in a professional healthcare setting rather than a traditional classroom or lab. Thus, a good deal of this CID research is drawn directly from a healthcare context. For instance, Brasseur (2012) discovered that sonographers experience communication challenges in the workplace that are not typically addressed in the traditional classroom or recognized in the official discourse of their profession. Such discoveries may not emerge in a survey where participants are merely asked to reflect on professional communication challenges. Essentially, even when industry professionals are asked to reflect on their experiences in interviews and surveys or are invited as guest critics to the academic design critique, the feedback provided is more academically idealized than it would be if drawn directly from a professional environment (Dannels, 2002; Dannels et al., 2003; Dannels & Gaffney, 2009; Dannels & Martin, 2008; Smith, 2005). Instructors with a connection to academia and students with internships and co-ops have an altered kind of professional pressure (split between different worlds) or a bias (unconscious or not) when it comes to their understanding of educational techniques, what higher education offers the workplace, and how communication is valued.

Optics, photonics, and communication

The optics and photonics industry is growing exponentially in many science and engineering fields such as health, computing, and security, among others (National Research Council, 2013). For example, medical technicians and doctors need a basic understanding of optics and photonics to interpret medical images and perform interventional radiology techniques. Since optics and photonics are rarely taught formally in the academy, companies must hire people with general science backgrounds in physics, chemistry, mechanical engineering, electrical engineering, computer science, and other STEM areas. Thus, optics and photonics is truly an integrated STEM field. To address this gap in specialized knowledge, millions of dollars are spent on training optics and photonics professionals (Empire State Development, March, 2018; Test, 2015). This education focuses on achieving both technical outcomes and outcomes associated with "integrated education, such as critical thinking, communication, teamwork, and abilities for lifelong learning" (NASEM, 2018, p. vii). Without an investigation into how communication is actually understood and used in the real workplace context, though, instruction designed to help socialize new employees could be highly disconnected from the actual communication challenges faced on a daily basis. Consequently, communication scholars may miss an opportunity to positively impact communication practices in this rapidly growing field. We argue that it is especially important to provide an in-depth investigation by communication scholars related to how employees become socialized into what it means to be a competent communicator. Thus, this study focuses on understanding the communication expectations of employers and the means by which entry-level employees are taught about them as part of the socialization process.

Therefore, we pose the following research questions:

(1) What characterizes competent communication in the optics and photonics workplace?
(2) How do optics and photonics professionals socialize members into the communication expectations of the field?

Methods

This research is the first phase of an ongoing NSF-funded study examining the optics and photonics workforce and how entry-level employees transfer their knowledge of math, physics, and communication into their work. The research team consists of communication, physics, and science education scholars. This study examines what and how employees learn about communication in a regional optics and photonics workforce. By situating our study within one geographic region, we were able to gain access to a tightly knit community of over 60 companies.

For this first phase of the study, we collected data at 15 different companies, all from one geographic region. These companies range in size from four to 200 employees and address a wealth of needs in various fields such as healthcare, information technology, and energy. We used an ethnographic interviewing framework (Spradley, 1979) to gather information from employees, managers, and hiring professionals (Miles & Huberman, 1984).

Setting

The optics and photonics industry is a diverse field that creates products with a wide range of applications such as small but very strong plastic lights used on the outside of airplanes, lenses in NASA telescopes, contact lenses, optical inspection systems for food packaging, and film-printing medical devices. The field is sometimes categorized as advanced manufacturing partly due to the range and types of employees. Optics and photonics companies have teams of engineers in charge of sales, research, and design, as well as another team of technicians who are tasked with making the finely crafted products. Technicians and engineers often work in different locations of the company building and are provided with different training and education opportunities.

Although there are exceptions, engineers are usually considered above technicians in the company's hierarchy. Most technician positions may require a high school diploma, and almost all engineering positions require a degree in engineering or another related field, like applied mathematics. If technicians pursue a 4-year degree and are proactive in seeking other kinds of training opportunities or leadership experiences, they may also move up from technician to engineer. Engineers may have additional leadership roles. These leading engineers are often described as "naturally good communicators."

In addition to the regional companies, the photonics and optics field also depends on academic research labs. Many regional companies maintain close relationships with researchers housed in universities, with managers of companies also teaching as adjuncts at these universities. Although two research labs were located within local universities and were not connected to a particular company, they were treated as part of the professional sample because the graduate assistants were treated as entry-level employees. Faculty and industry managers were asked similar questions that focused on the skills they most desired for their research assistants.

Data and participants

For this first phase of the study, we interviewed a total of 33 participants—18 managers (16 industry, 2 academic labs), 14 entry-level employees (11 industry and 3 academic research assistants) and one hiring manager (see Table 1) from 15 local companies in the photonics and optics field (see Table 2). Although we did not ask participants to identify their gender, of the 33 participants we interviewed, 5 self-presented as women, and 28 self-presented as men (see Table 1). Prior to conducting interviews, we obtained permission from the Institution Review Board, and participants were provided information about this approval and their rights as human subjects.

Companies were included in the sample if their work was related to optics and/or photonics. Company gatekeepers were solicited via email to inquire about participation in the study. If a company agreed, we solicited individual employee interviews either directly via email or through the company gatekeeper. Participants were offered a small monetary incentive to participate in an interview. We also solicited participants through local community organizations such as the Optical Society of America.

Participants provided informed consent to audio-record their interviews. The interview protocol (see Appendix) focused on what employers want students to know or to be able to do when they enter the workforce. Included in the protocol were several questions specific

Table 1. Participant demographics.

Sector	Position	Men	Women
Education	Associate Professor	2	
	Graduate Research Assistant	2	1
Industry	Technician	4	1
	Engineer/Scientist	5	1
	Manager	14	2
	HR Manager	1	0

Table 2. Participant company/research group focus.

Sector	Focus	Number of participants
Education	Spectroscopic diagnostics	3
	Opto-electronics/Photonics packaging	2
Industry	Precision optics manufacturing (glass)	8
	Precision optics manufacturing (polymers, ceramics, specialty)	8
	Image/lighting systems (projectors, organic light emitting diodes, lasers)	6
	Precision optical fabrication machines and metrology systems	4
	Opto-electronics/Photonics packaging	2

about communication, such as: What communication tasks/situations (e.g., making presentations to clients, writing internal reports, summarizing research) do employees take part in in daily/weekly (routine tasks)? Which of these types of tasks do you expect employees to have experienced prior to employment? What have you noticed about communication strengths or weaknesses of new hires? What are the trends? What training opportunities, if any, exist to help employees develop communication abilities on the job? We included follow-up questions when appropriate and when time would allow. These interviews were transcribed using TranscribeMe, and imported into NVivo. The average interview length was 59 min, and the 33 interviews resulted in a total of 1957 min (32 hr 37 min) of data. Within NVivo, the data were broken into units and were coded for this project if related to communication.

Data analysis

We analyzed the transcripts entered into Nvivo using a typological analysis framework consisting of three main steps (Goetz & LeCompte, 1984; Miles & Huberman, 1984). The first step involved reviewing the data and coding the interview responses to one or more of the research questions. Although the larger study involved research questions focused on skills related to physics and math, we only report on the data as related to the communication research questions. This process resulted in 1,493 communication codes or data units. The second step utilized constant comparative analysis (Glaser & Straus, 1967; Goetz & LeCompte, 1984; LeCompte & Preissle, 1993; Miles & Huberman, 1984; Patton, 1980; Strauss & Corbin, 1994). We compared categories that emerged as a result of the data analysis (Dey, 1993; Patton, 1990). As a research team, we reflected on our notes and observations from the interviews and began to develop categories that we labeled in NVivo. We analyzed all of the communication-coded data again with these newly developed categories. Then, we clustered these categories into themes depending on how our specific research questions related to communication (Dey, 1993; Glaser & Straus, 1967; Goetz & LeCompte, 1984; LeCompte & Preissle, 1993; Miles & Huberman, 1984; Patton, 1980; Strauss & Corbin, 1994).

These themes were collaboratively reviewed by a team of six coders. Through discussion, we arrived at operational definitions for each theme. After refining the themes, we recoded a subset of the data based on our operational definitions and compared our coding results. In order to further validate our coding, we gave a subset of the data to an independent coder with less familiarity with the data. We asked her to code units into the predefined themes and she was able to utilize our operational definitions to code the units reliably (Cohen's kappa = .89).[2] Finally, the third step of the typological analysis framework involved drawing conclusions based on the themes identified in relationship to the research questions (Goetz & LeCompte, 1984; Miles & Huberman, 1984).

Results

Statements from participants reveal that competent communication in the optics and photonics workplace consists of recognizing the complexity of a rhetorical situation and making socially acceptable communicative decisions for a particular organizational culture. However, the ways in which members of these workplaces are socialized into the communication norms varied widely, often depending on the role of the employee.

RQ1: competent communication in optics/photonics workplaces

The following section describes five prevalent themes—proactive questioning, efficient decision-making, familial-like humor, tactful translation, and fluent modality switching—that emerged from the data related to how optics and photonics employees identified strong communicators.

Proactive questioning. Asking questions was one of the most frequent actions identified by employees. It was especially important in regard to the mentor–mentee relationship. Some employees are hired based on the kinds of questions they ask during the interview. Even when managers and entry-level employees discuss training unrelated to communication, they often mention how trainees have greater success when they proactively ask questions. One engineer, Brady, explained the importance of asking questions:

> And you also learn to ask more questions than you've done previously. If you don't understand something you ask it. You don't try to figure it out on your own because you don't want to mess around with company funding.

In this instance, Brady shows that proactive question asking is valuable, as it saves time and money. Another technician, Antoni, affirmed the importance of asking questions in a timely manner:

> Yes, asking questions, having that communication, talking to their peers, talking to their supervisor, and not waiting until like, "Okay, I need this by next Wednesday." Then regurgitating it up, and then having it not be even close to what was …

In addition to saving time, Chip suggested that asking questions can be beneficial, as it shows a potential new hire's initiative:

> But another thing that I looked for is whether or not a person is smart enough and takes enough initiative to go see what's new in the literature … that's where a lot of that is, is getting out and taking the initiative and then going and talking, "I read this, what is … " you know, "I have a question about this," or whatever. But that is another thing to look for in potential hires.

Overall asking questions can help a company, but someone who is proactive in asking questions requires time as an investment. Jacob acknowledged the time it takes to work with someone who asks questions and how it contributes to success in the long run:

> When we're working with people, you have the type of people that are going to ask a million questions and they're inquisitive and they want to know all the minute details that go into the

> process and those tend to take a little bit longer. People like that tend to take a little bit longer to train, but in the long run they tend to be some of the best opticians that we've ever had ...

As illustrated, asking proactive questions is not only about clarifying information, but also about learning cultural norms regarding what is appropriate and the value placed on time and effort. Waiting and being timid are equated with "messing around with company funding." Understanding technical information in-depth (through questioning) is also seen as building strength among employees and trustworthiness of the company.

Efficient decision-making

Proactive questions and information seeking also contributed to efficient decision-making. Both managers and entry-level employees became frustrated if someone took too long or felt uncomfortable making a decision. Interviewees agreed that failing to commit was worse than making a wrong decision. Vina explained that the culture of a fast-moving technological industry requires employees to be efficient, even if this means failing sometimes:

> Yeah, willingness to work independently and with a team, a willingness to accept failure. Optics manufacturing is the constant development of new processes, nothing's set in stone. We're always looking to be more efficient and better.

Lee also described making quick decisions in order to move efficiently as part of the culture of optics and photonics:

> That's the culture. You've got to be very versatile in what you do in optics, because the gears switch constantly and continually. You've got to be able to adapt to that. You can't get on one path and think you're safe, because you can get tripped up in a heartbeat by customer expectation or something else, and you have to switch gears quickly. You have to do it efficiently and without argument.

When there are breakdowns in efficiency, entry-level employees have to find alternative ways to communicate. Jordan recounted an incident when he needed an answer to move forward:

> So I will say email is definitely not the fastest thing over there. Because I remember when I was talking to the production manager it took weeks between emails and I was like, you know what? I'm not going to wait anymore. I'll just go and give them a call.

Like being timid about decision-making, regret was also frowned upon. All levels of employees appreciated the importance of being decisive and resolving loose ends. In this example, Maria affirmed the irritation of the industry with wasted time while making decisions:

> There's always decisions to be made ... When do you need to get the next person involved? Make that decision and feel comfortable with it. Because even if you make the wrong decision at least you just didn't do nothing because that's the worst thing.

As with proactively asking questions, the problem with failing to take initiative and moving forward is that time is wasted. Inefficient decision-making has an even greater potential to diminish productivity.

Familial-like humor. Employees' discussion about communication routinely mentioned the advantage of learning about the personality of the company, fitting in with the company culture, and consequently communicating the same sense of humor and commitment to the team.

The following statements reveal that, for many of the optics and photonics companies, if the job candidate or new employee appears too rigid or humorless, he or she will likely not fit with the organizational culture. The organizational culture is not always inclusive or equitable, in some instances even referred to as a "boys club." Being able to relax and joke with friends was a desirable trait. For example, Daniil, an entry-level employee, described how humor affected his experience in the workplace:

> Yes, so that's one of the things I really like about this company is that I feel like I fit in really well. The group of people we have here is really good. ... I don't know, we just joke around a lot. Easy to get along with. Kind of have similar interests. We do a lot of practical jokes on each other. ... It's a joking kind of community.

In this case, fitting in means being able to joke around together. Atlas, an entry-level employee from a different company, described a very similar work environment:

> You've got to be able to joke around. That's a big deal. Coming from any job that I've had, people that really don't joke around, nobody really involves them with stuff, because they feel like they're uptight, or they're going to say something to management. If someone says something that they don't like, people tend to shy away. See, I'm more of a social person. So, I'm able to go in there and actually talk to people, and joke around, and be able to talk to people.

For Atlas, being social and accepted by others meant being able to joke around. Sascha also felt that finding a way to engage with workplace humor was necessary for being included:

> In a more casual sense it definitely took a while to feel like I fit in because there'd be engineer happy hours, and then people would go to make jokes and would be like, "You can't say that there's a girl here." And I'm like, "Shut-up. I'll tell you if I'm offended." ... Because I finally went to one of the engineer happy hours, and someone was like, "You can't make that joke." And I was like, "No. You can make that joke. I was thinking the punch-line to that joke."

In order to become part of the group, not only did Sascha have to join a culture of joking around, but she had to explicitly acknowledge that she was not offended by the jokes. The emphasis on humor was consistent through the ranks, with one technician mentioning, "My supervisor will always play pranks when he sees people are too serious ... " In this instance, the supervisor actively encouraged joking behaviors. Another manager actively developed a joking culture by looking for similar qualities during interviews with potential hires:

> Are they someone that is going to get along with people here? Do they have a personality that can joke around with people and have a good attitude and good team player type personality, or are they going to just want to sit in their cubicle all day and eat lunch at their desk by themselves every day versus everyone else who eats lunch together in the break room or eats lunch together out at a picnic table outside.

Thus, for these companies, the ideal communicator is someone who is outgoing and has a casual sense of humor and is easy to get along with, even regarding practical jokes and pranks.

Tactful translation. Being able to translate information from one group to another within and outside of the company was highly valued, but there was always a focus on respect and tact during the translation process. Managers recognized the necessity of this kind of communication because, without it, their main goals could never be efficiently realized. For example, Parker illustrated what can go wrong when one group fails to translate tactfully across occupations:

> A lot of times, us in engineering and manufacturing often want the same thing but ... there are several different approaches and if one of those two groups can make a real small change and make have a big impact on the other, a lot of times that's not easily seen. ... Just the other day ... we found this issue in software. ... And all these steps on the software side of things are easy but to implement them over in manufacturing is difficult. So manufacturing blew up and said, "All of this is our fault ... "

Employees in the optics and photonics workforce regard tactful translational communication that cuts across occupations as especially necessary for those in leadership positions. Managers complain about engineers' conveying messages infrequently to technicians or using abrupt or inconsiderate language over the phone or when emailing. As Barry explained,

> We do check and adjust along the way but there's still—it's about knowing your audience as well. What does this person want? They don't want a bunch of fluff, then don't give it to them. I just—I read it [email to technician], and I'm like, "Oh, I wouldn't want an email like that." Brutal honesty is okay, but you can also make it tactful, I think.

In another example, Cole, a manager who had witnessed a lot of changes in the company's size and greater emphasis on academic credentials and hierarchy, referred to employees as being in a familial relationship where respect is key to the group dynamic:

> The ability of people to work with people at all levels of education, right? Because we're a small facility here. Unlike [Name of company] where development's done in the research lab, and engineering's done in a different building, and the factory's somewhere else in the world, we all live together. So, you've got to be able to talk to the technician running the machine that has maybe a two-year degree, maybe not. You've got to be able to communicate with him respectfully, you've got to trust that they have a certain level of understanding of the process, and be able to transfer your knowledge to them. An engineer that looks down at people without the right degree is not going to succeed.

In these situations, part of the ideal kind of translation would include a gentler approach. As efficiency is important, the manager in this recent example reveals how brutal honesty can be helpful but points out how tact can actually contribute to a more positive exchange of ideas. Perhaps Raleigh put it best when he explained the practice of documenting work with a respect not just for the people involved, but for the company itself and its larger goals:

> [You] need to record all the information accurately, organized legibly [laughter]. These are important things. It has to be structured in a way that a person who—we always use this analogy—if they get hit by a bus, somebody can come the next day and pick up where they left off and keep going.

Fluent modality switching. The optics and photonics field often includes small to medium-sized companies where employees might be asked to perform a range of jobs depending on the type of project the company secures. Many companies ask their employees to become acquainted with a variety of positions and communication modes (phone etiquette especially with customers, presentations, documenting on Excel, email, etc.) in order to understand the perspectives of different departments. Even in situations where employees' tasks and position remain fairly regular, they will likely be communicating with a variety of groups with a variety of communication needs and desired modes of delivery. As Howard indicated, choosing the most appropriate channel for communicating can be challenging:

> What we find as I'm moving into the older part of the workforce is that the young kids—I call them kids. The youngsters in their 20s that work for me, they like to rely more and more on digital media for communication than they do face-to-face or telephone. And what I get a lot from my team is, "Oh, I sent them an email." And my response is generally, "Please pick up the phone and call them because they might not answer your email for a couple of hours. If there's something you need to get done, go ahead and send your email, if don't get a response in a couple hours, pick up the phone." And so, a lot of the younger generation will prefer to just rely on the nonverbal communication.

In this case, the manager sees a reluctance to speak with people face-to-face or over the phone. Even when the interaction is face to face, employees may need to use multiple modes of communication, as suggested by Alex:

> When I see somebody or am working with somebody in another area, I try to instruct them, make some examples, show them some issues, maybe doing some drawing on a whiteboard, things like that, instead of just quick, off-the-cuff, back-of-a-napkin type of stuff.

In fact, choosing the most appropriate manner to send a message is often as important as the message itself. In the following example, the managers require employees to create a PowerPoint for presentations or updates with the senior staff. Although the PowerPoint might take more time to create, getting the message clearly communicated to the senior staff, and in a mode they anticipate, can be beneficial for the company.

> When we do updates a lot of times for senior staff, there'll be project updates that require PowerPoint. The interns that I'd spoke about previously, they all had to do a PowerPoint on what they did for the summer, what they learned, what they thought they were going to learn but didn't get, what was good about our PL and what they would like to see for future interns.

In addition to PowerPoint presentations, members of this industry often use video to communicate an idea. As Joseph suggested:

> A lot of times we'll take videos of us doing some function with our tools, send that to them and they can repeat what we did to train them. We'll fly across the world to do training on-site and to set up these systems. So you have to be able to travel and speak in front of groups of 20–25 people.

Jamie emphasized the importance of making a message easily accessible to a customer, whether that means using PowerPoint or simply being a strong public speaker:

> Again, some people are better at it than others and more comfortable, whether it's public speaking or whether it's being able to have a clear message on a PowerPoint. When you go present something to a customer, it's nice to have a PowerPoint that everyone can follow, and they can keep a copy of it, and they can refer to it, and it has all the—yeah, and everyone needs to really have it because whether it's a PowerPoint that does something in sales or whether it's a PowerPoint that solves a problem for engineering, or some kind of design, it's kind of nice to be able to have that. They walk through that step-by-step process and be able to create that and present it to their customer.

Managers cultivate their employees' ability to choose among multiple modes of communication and become fluent, even when they bemoan the lack of employees' basic skills across all of these modalities. When a new employee enters the workplace already strong in these areas and is able to make good choices among these modalities without prompting, that employee is praised and often identified as a candidate for a leadership position.

RQ2: socialization into communication expectations

The second research question focused on how members of these communities socialized each other (and, in particular, how managers socialized entry-level employees) into the communication norms in the optics and photonics workplace. Generally, how and to what extent communication was explicitly taught often depended on the employee's role; but in general, communication instruction was articulated as something that should have already been learned through previous experiences, through their high school, or possibly within undergraduate education. Once at the company, most of the communication training occurred through informal channels (such as informal mentoring). The exception to this was with the engineers; for those identified as likely future leaders, formal communication training was much more likely. Hence, the hierarchical structures often determined the kinds of communication socialization that occurred—whether it did not occur because of presumed communication competence or whether it occurred in more informal mentoring or structured training sessions.

Presumed communication competence. Employers often mentioned that they expected employees to already have particular communication abilities. Sometimes, someone would not be hired based on performance in an interview or the person would be hired with a sink or swim mentality. In other words, a person with lower communication skills was hired with the understanding that the hire would not last long if he or she did not adapt as needed and adapt quickly. Responses illustrating this were often short; for example, managers would say, "we don't provide training for that right now," or something like "people learn that on the job if they need to. For the most part, many of the people come in with that skill." Similarly managers said they would not hire someone, "no matter how good he [sic] is, unless he [sic] can talk."

On the one hand, most supervisors and entry-level employees acknowledged that communication "can be learned," but these statements were often paired with how strong communication abilities came naturally to some: "I hate to say I think some of it's just natural, but it can be learned," or, "It can be taught, but at the same time, I think some of it is just a natural ability." Other times, communication was described as something that employees should already have mastered by the time they arrive at their company, as one manager implied when he said, "Just basic skills, basic communications skills that you learn when you're a little kid."

These conflicting statements suggest that, although communication was often described as easy to learn, employers considered communication to be something that employees should already have mastered by the time they arrived at their company. They also acknowledged how their company's success relied on strong communication and that many provided minimal training to develop this essential and critical skill. In short, communication was both highly valued and seen as something that all companies were not necessarily willing (or able) to teach or develop. It was considered something anyone could do (we learn to speak at a very young age) and something only a select group of people were born with (in terms of innate expertise).

Informal mentoring. Both engineers and technicians in the optics and photonics workplace had some kind of mentoring or apprenticeship experience when learning about their roles in the company. Although technicians were not provided formal opportunities to advance their communication abilities, they (as well as engineers) were often provided opportunities to communicate within their groups and receive feedback from immediate supervisors. Employees commonly participated in "rotations," where new employees worked in or rotated through multiple divisions for a set period of time to learn what was required across many positions. These rotations also gave new employees opportunities to experience how people across divisions communicated. Entry-level technicians often received training from more senior-level technicians and engineers, while graduate students received training from more senior-level technicians or faculty. Although communication scenarios for graduate students in optics and photonics were even more infrequent than for industry engineers, Conrad told us about practicing for an upcoming conference and receiving feedback from an audience he could "corral" into listening:

> So, I actually just went to a conference in February and it was a lot of, a couple of weeks before the conference, making a first sort of mockup of the PowerPoint and practicing it in front of [mentor] and other lab members and whoever we could sort of corral into coming and them giving a bunch of feedback like, "okay, you sort of rushed through this part, explain this part better, don't go into so much detail about that."

Oral feedback and sharing communication knowledge from years of experience were some of the most common ways of socializing employees. In this example, Trey talked about how experience helps develop an understanding of the importance of audience analysis:

> So, knowing who your audience is and what you want your outcome to be from that meeting, and … what your audience might be looking for. We can definitely mentor them. And they wouldn't have the experience that we would have.

Another manager, Van, explained the company process of providing feedback after talking with customers on the phone:

> And then when it comes to talking to customers, myself or one of the other experienced engineers will sit with the new guy or girl for the first telephone call that they do, or the first online meeting that they do and provide feedback as to what they did good, what could have been improved, what was clear, what was confusing. And then just kind of incrementally give them more and more freedom and until you just let them go until they can do it autonomously basically.

As part of the informal mentor–mentee training, many of the technicians received years of instruction from a trainer or supervisor, but sometimes never direct instruction about communication. Instead, entry-level employees received directives about their responsibilities more generally. Communication norms, preferences, and styles were learned by observation within the training and through "doing." Part of that "doing" had to be prompted by employees through their own initiative, as another manager Dominic explained:

> And so it's mentoring. And like I said, if they really got into it and they really wanted to do more, then we could do additional training if they wanted. You know, if they were a permanent employee.

When it came to competency in group communication, even informal mentoring was neglected. Employees were given opportunities to work in a team but had to work together to determine how to keep everyone on task and manage conflict among personalities.

> Right now we're working on a training process with an extremely abrasive personality in the group, and we're all just trying to learn how to work together, and keep everybody on track, and not let one person just take over. You have to learn how to balance the group.

Although opportunities to participate at conferences or in larger group or sales meetings were not available to technicians (like for the engineers), technicians were asked to help support each other on the production floor where communication was pervasive due to frequent question asking, team communication, and documentation.

Structured instruction for leading engineers. Small to midsized companies spent a large amount of time and money training employees about the technical aspects of their roles. In fact, many managers noted the way in which their company products were so specialized it would be unreasonable to assume students could acquire the knowledge or skills externally (hence, they have to train them). However, when managers and entry-level employees were asked about formal communication training, their answers revealed that formal training was primarily for the engineers, not the technicians. Commonly, participants shared comments like, "Nobody on the floor really receives communication training, except maybe if you're going to move on to an engineer or trainer, but that's about it." For example, Jase (a manager) discussed a formal training program designed for "influential" engineers:

> Yeah. So we try to recognize that we've just completed a pretty—I would say intense—coaching program here for influential folks. So our team leaders, we brought somebody in to work on, A, self-awareness but also how to communicate and adapt your style to other styles both written and verbally.

Another manager, Nicole, confessed that she wished employees became better at documenting in their undergraduate experience, but expected them to be formally trained while at the company:

> Well documentation, that is something that I would hope that they would learn [chuckles] in school in their undergraduate. However that's not necessarily the case, and so it's just it has to be an expectation here at [name of company]. ... What we do as well is, we offer a lot of training in house. We actually just offered a grant writing class. We've had technical writing classes.

Brendan, another manager, described his company's willingness to train engineers in interpersonal skills and conflict management strategies:

> Yes. They'll usually be at one of the local hotels or something where they have a conference room for a couple of days. We're willing to do that. That's not a problem. For our group leaders, supervisors, we try to do those one and two-day programs that they offer. Very similar, I can't remember what the names of the companies are. But it's usually somebody who's been in the industry for years and they teach you. It's interpersonal skills and how you manage and how do you deal with difficult personalities. Things like that.

Engineers in these companies often worked in sales but the bulk of their previous formal education was in STEM content-knowledge and not in the education outcomes associated with "integrated education" like communication. Akeno, a manager, revealed this understanding and the company's solution:

> Sure, yes. We've brought in sales training for—like I said, most of the people who come in the door of our sales team, they're not salesmen, they're scientists. So we bring in sales trainers. We've brought in the past to help them learn some of the techniques of being an effective salesman, some the steps that you need to take.

Many of these statements also reveal that engineers were given additional opportunities but especially those engineers that were currently in a leadership position or had the potential for leadership. Participants mentioned "influential folks," "group leaders," and "supervisors" as targeted employees for receiving the training.

The results from RQ2 point to a hierarchy of instruction that differentiates employees based on presumed skill and perceived promise. Many of these companies expected employees to come into the job with a firm grasp on communication skills based on education or previous experience; they mentored broadly (which may or may not have included communication); and they offered structured learning opportunities for the employees seen as future leaders.

CID in the optics and photonics workplace: developing cross-occupational communication competence

Essential to growing the organizations in this study and lauded as highly valuable by management was the ability to communicate between novice and expert, between technician and engineer, between employee and customer. This analysis revealed that effective communication required more than simply translating a message. Requiring a combination of translation, fluent modality switching, cultural appropriateness and efficiency, effective communication involved what we refer to as *cross-occupational communication*. We define cross-occupational communication as an interactive, iterative process involving communicative needs assessment, information exchange, and rhetorical/situational flexibility with employees distinct in background, training, and occupational roles.

To expand (and based on the results of this study), cross-occupational communication necessitates that the communicator must understand the communicative needs of those who might not have shared expertise or job descriptions and then exchange messages in a respectful way that advances positive interpersonal relationships and considers the complexity of the context and the occupational roles of those involved. For example, a metrology engineer responsible for testing described needing to be able to communicate with an optical engineer in a different division in order to troubleshoot the system he was trying to build:

> I've built a couple of systems and it was going great, and then every now and then something just doesn't behave right. And so it's just kind of looking at the model, talking to the optical engineers seeing, okay this is how I should expect this thing to move.

It is often difficult for technicians and engineers to work together solving problems, because of differences in education backgrounds and the complexity involved in company hierarchies; yet, employees say that communicating respectfully across such differences is essential. A manager emphasized this importance of cross-occupational communication when he explained:

> You can't just simply go to a mechanical person all the time to get a mechanical answer and an optics person all the time to get an optics answer. And you need to be able to talk with people who are subject matter experts and know how to ask the right questions and know how to understand what they're saying.

Understanding the needs of those who might not have the same expertise is especially important when communicating mathematics. For example,

> When you throw up some graphs on an Excel spreadsheet or on a PowerPoint presentation, they might make sense to you because you've stared at them for a couple hours, but trying to get the idea of how people seeing for the first time are going to take them really matters a lot, and that's something that no one really ever teaches you. You have to kind of gauge people's reactions to things that you've shown them in the past and say, "Okay, well he thought that this color being red meant it was bad, so maybe I should try to make it green."

There are cultural subtleties that communicators need to take into account, especially when working with customers.

Cross-occupational communication, then, suggests a broader view of communication focused not only on the message but also on the appropriateness of communication to the occupational role of the audience and to the organizational culture. As seen in the first quote of this paper, employees need to be aware of an audience's level of technical understanding while respecting intelligence. They need to understand that senior personnel will prefer a PowerPoint during a presentation to share information more quickly, or grasp that customers or vendors will prefer a phone call as opposed to an email. Although primary communicative goals might be about shared information related to completing a project (i.e., "task mastery" in the socialization literature), equally important (even if unspoken) goals involve garnering support and buy-in from disparate groups within and outside of the company. This necessitates more than information exchange.

The question then becomes: to what extent can companies develop cross-occupational communication competence and to what end? While many socialization processes in these companies occurred informally, employees did learn about industry-specific communication norms and expectations and were able to articulate them as nuanced, not formulaic. Furthermore, these socialization processes were not necessarily only about holistically advancing the individual and their communication abilities but also about developing employees' organizational commitment. While only some employees received formal communication instruction, all employees took part in various socialization activities that both cultivated and reinforced the idea that good communication is about doing what's best for the company (not just doing what is best for the employee). Documentation should be clear for the next person who may work on a project, and presentations have to be professional to impress clients. Colleagues should have a good sense of humor or laid back attitude, contributing to a positive workplace environment that motivates people to continue working. Hence, the outcomes of communication socialization in these companies were not solely about individual professional development; rather, they involved commitment and organizational efficiency and success.

Implications for teaching in the workplace

Two different meta-analyses (Bauer et al., 2007; Saks et al., 2007) have shown that a CID approach to both mentoring and other formal tactics would likely help with retention and role clarity. Most CID research has focused primarily on communication instruction in academic contexts (e.g., Dannels, 2002; Dannels et al., 2003; Dannels & Gaffney, 2009; Dannels & Martin, 2008; Smith, 2005). Yet this research also acknowledges the challenges with trying to simulate workplace contexts within the classroom (Dannels & Martin, 2008). Students and faculty don't fully commit to the professional nature of the experience, and preprofessional socialization is complicated by feedback provided to students that is "reflective of academic developmental stages or idealized workplace contexts than of actual professional settings" (p. 135).

We argue that in some cases in certain professional fields, systematic CID instruction that takes place within the workforce and that focuses on the complex company-specific or field-specific communication practices is needed. For instance, based on this study, cross-occupational communication competence—an interactive, iterative process involving communicative needs assessment, information exchange, and rhetorical/situational flexibility with groups distinct in background, training, and occupational role—may be incredibly important for the optics and photonics field, but might not carry the same weight in a much different type of STEM industry.

Admittedly, communication education within the workplace comes in a variety of forms. Some companies might have relationships with CID scholars and graduate students who would also like access to a professional context for research but could offer CID instruction to entry-level employees. In this model, the CID scholar would first conduct a study like the one here to determine how the regional workplace characterizes competent communication. Then, that scholar (and possibly other expert communication consultants trained by the CID scholar) could observe various rhetorical situations as they occur and provide feedback and suggestions. Or, the CID scholar could design various communication training modules and simulations developed by observing actual scenarios. These modules and simulations could be later implemented by other trainers within the company. These modules could also involve relationships with communication centers or departments at universities where company trainers could take workshops related to socializing new employees by teaching the complexity of communication. Workplace contexts for popular local industries could also be simulated in these communication centers or labs at universities. This approach is already used in preprofessional disciplines like nursing. For faculty teaching in disciplines where students might go into a number of fields, exposing them to a variety of likely workplace contexts would provide them experience of translating communication knowledge in various rhetorical situations. In addition to inviting faculty into the classroom, finding opportunities where students can observe communication taking place in the company or participating in training programs prior to graduation might give them a better sense and appreciation of the rhetorical situations employees face.

Limitations and future research

This study was limited by its focus on employees in a singular geographic area. Additionally, only a few of the interview questions focused specifically on communication. The sample was also heavily skewed in terms of gender, which is largely reflective of the overall field. Future research should continue to focus on the optics and photonics field, but ought to be expanded to include training technicians in local high school programs, since this is where a lot of technicians receive a majority of their training prior to entering the workforce. Finally, formalized CID instruction ought to occur regularly within the workplace as a part of the socialization of entry-level employees.

Conclusion

Kedrowicz and Taylor (2013) charged CID scholars to treat communication as a "complex process understood as the interplay between audience, context, and purpose" (p. 96) as opposed to "a skill to accomplish professional goals." Instead of a "structural/functional transmission view of communication," the emphasis should be on "communication as social interaction and meaning" (p. 95). Although optics and photonics employees in this study, like the engineers described by Kedrowicz and Taylor (2013), describe communication as a means to an end, their in-depth explanations suggest they can and do appreciate communication as a complex and sophisticated process with social and relational implications. If they understand communication in this way, shouldn't we teach and train them accordingly?

Although much of this teaching and training happens in academic settings, the simulated workplaces are insufficient for preparing future employees for these communication complexities in the workplace. For employees in this study, the repercussions of their success (or failure) in communication were very real. These kinds of high-stakes experiences are difficult or impossible to prepare for. That does not mean, though, that we should not try in academia or that we should depend solely on on-the-job trial and error. Rather, we should consider seriously what industry-specific, value-added communication training could benefit various workplaces and how we can best bring our scholarly expertise to the task. Practical training in workplace contexts is important in learning professional, discipline-specific communication competence. Thus, a logical avenue for future exploration would be exploring new methods of CID training and scholarship within the workplace, as an extension or a transition from higher education. In workplaces where "spewing nonsense" has ramifications beyond information exchange, understanding and teaching communication as a complex negotiation of individual needs, relational hierarchies, organizational contexts, and rhetorical situations has the potential to benefit all involved.

Funding

This work was supported by National Science Foundation (NSF) [Grant Number DGE-1432578].

Notes

1. Schaufeli and Bakker (2010) define this concept of "affective-motivational state of high energy" in two parts: first, "affective" as a "personal sense of belonging, pride, attachment, inspiration, affirmation from work and being part of the organization" and, second, "motivation" as "the drive to perform a high standard."
2. Although debate exists about the value of intercoder reliability in qualitative research, many researchers believe it can support validity in analyzing open-ended interview data (Kurasaki, 2000).

References

Antonacopoulou, E. P., & Güttel, W. H. (2010). Staff induction practices and organizational socialization: A review and extension of the debate. *Society and Business Review*, 5(1), 22–47.

Batistič, S., & Kaše, R. (2015). The organizational socialization field fragmentation: A bibliometric review. *Scientometrics*, 104(1), 121–146.

Bauer, T. N., Bodner, T., Erdogan, B., Truxillo, D. M., & Tucker, J. S. (2007). Newcomer adjustment during organizational socialization: A meta-analytic review of antecedents, outcomes, and methods. *Journal of Applied Psychology*, 92(3), 707–721. doi:10.1037/0021-9010.92.3.707

Bousaba, N. A., Conrad, J. M., Coco, J. L., Cox, R. W., & Miri, M. (2014, June 15–18). *Incorporating oral presentations into electrical and computer engineering design courses: A four-course study*. 121st ASEE annual conference & exposition.

Brasseur, L. (2012). Sonographers' complex communication during the obstetric sonogram exam: An interview study. *Journal of Technical Writing and Communication*, 42(1), 3–19. doi:10.2190/TW.42.1.b

Canary, H. E., Ellison, K., Herkert, J. R., Tarin, C. A., Taylor, J. L., & Wetmore, J. M. (2014). Engaging students in integrated ethics education: A communication in the disciplines study of pedagogy and students' roles in society. *Communication Education*, 63, 83–104.

Carnevale, A. P., Smith, D., & Melton, M. (2011). *Stem: Science, technology, engineering, mathematics*. Washington, DC: Georgetown University Center on Education and the Workforce.

Commeiras, N., Loubes, A., & Bories-Azeau, I. (2013). Identification of organizational socialization tactics: The case of sales and marketing trainees in higher education. *European Management Journal*, 31(2), 164–178.

Committee on Prospering in the Global Economy of the 21st Century: An Agenda for American Science and Technology, National Academy of Sciences, National Academy of Engineering, & Institute of Medicine (US). (2007). *Rising above the gathering storm: Energizing and employing America for a brighter economic future*. Washington, DC: National Academies Press.

Cyphert, D. (2002). Integrating communication across the MBA curriculum. *Business Communication Quarterly*, 65, 81–86.

Dannels, D. P. (2001). Time to speak up: A theoretical framework of situated pedagogy and practice for communication across the curriculum. *Communication Education*, 50, 144–158.

Dannels, D. P. (2002). Communication across the curriculum and in the disciplines: Speaking in engineering. *Communication Education*, 51, 254–268.

Dannels, D. P. (2003). Teaching and learning design presentations in engineering: Contradictions between academic and workplace activity systems. *Journal of Business and Technical Communication*, 17, 139–169.

Dannels, D. P. (2005). Performing tribal rituals: A genre analysis of "crits" in design studios. *Communication Education*, 54, 136–160.

Dannels, D. P., Anson, C. M., Bullard, L., & Peretti, S. (2003). Challenges in learning communication skills in chemical engineering. *Communication Education*, 52, 50–56.

Dannels, D. P., Gaffney, A. H., & Martin, K. N. (2008). Beyond content, deeper than delivery: What critique feedback reflects about communication expectations in design education. *International Journal of SoTL*, 2(2). Retrieved from http://academics.georgiasouthern.edu/ijsotl/v2n2.html

Dannels, D. P., & Gaffney, A. L. (2009). Communication across the curriculum and in the disciplines: A call for scholarly cross-cultural advocacy. *Communication Education*, 58, 124–153.

Dannels, D. P., & Martin, K. (2008). Critiquing critiques: A genre analysis of feedback across novice to expert design studios. *Journal of Business and Technical Communication*, 22(2), 135–159.

Darling, A. L. (2005). Public presentations in mechanical engineering and the discourse of technology. *Communication Education*, 54, 20–33.

Darling, A. L., & Dannels, D. P. (2003). Practicing engineers talk about the importance of talk: A report on the role of oral communication in the workplace. *Communication Education*, 52, 1–16.

Dey, I. (1993). *Qualitative data analysis. A user friendly guide for social scientists*. London & New York: Routledge.

Empire State Development. (2018, March). Optics and imaging. Retrieved from https://esd.ny.gov/tags/industry/optics-and-imaging

Fabris, C. (2015, January). College students think they're ready for the workforce. Employers aren't so sure. *The Chronicle of Higher Education*. Retrieved from http://chronicle.com

Glaser, B. G., & Straus, A. L. (1967). *The discovery of grounded theory*. Chicago: Aldine.

Goetz, J., & LeCompte, M. (1984). *Ethnography and qualitative design in educational research*. Orlando, FL: Academic Press.

Haber, R. J., & Lingard, L. (2001). Learning oral presentation skills: A rhetorical analysis with pedagogical and professional implications. *Journal of General Internal Medicine, 16*, 308–314.

Hyvärinen, M. L., Isotalus, P., Katajavuori, N., & Tanskanen, P. (2010). A method for teaching communication in pharmacy in authentic work situations. *Communication Education, 59*, 124–145.

Hyvärinen, M. L., Isotalus, P., Katajavuori, N., & Tanskanen, P. (2012). Evaluating the use of criteria for assessing profession-specific communication skills in pharmacy. *Studies in Higher Education, 37*(3), 291–308.

Jones, G. R. (1986). Socialization tactics, self-efficacy, and newcomers' adjustments to organizations. *Academy of Management Journal, 29*(2), 262–279.

Katz, R. (1980). Time and work: Toward an integrative perspective (B. M. Staw & L. L. Cummings, Eds.). *Research in Organizational Behavior, 2*, 81–127.

Kedrowicz, A. (2015). Clients and veterinarians as partners in problem solving during cancer management: Implications for veterinary education. *Journal of Veterinary Medicine Education, 42*(4), 373–381.

Kedrowicz, A. A., Fish, R. E., & Hammond, S. (2015). Relationship between anticipatory socialization experiences and first-year veterinary students' career interests. *Journal of Veterinary Medicine Education, 42*(1), 18–27.

Kedrowicz, A. A., & Taylor, J. L. (2013). Engineering communication and the global workplace: Preparing professionals and global citizens. *Connexions: International Professional Communication Journal, 1*, 81–105.

Kowtha, N. R. (2018). Organizational socialization of newcomers: The role of professional socialization. *International Journal of Training and Development, 22*(2), 87–106.

Kurasaki, K. S. (2000). Intercoder reliability for validating conclusions drawn from open-ended interview data. *Field Methods, 12*(3), 179–194.

LeCompte, M. D., & Preissle, J. (1993). *Ethnography and qualitative design in educational research* (2nd ed). Boston: Academic Press.

Lingard, L., Garwood, K., Schryer, C. F., & Spafford, M. M. (2003). A certain art of uncertainty: Case presentation and the development of professional identity. *Social Science & Medicine, 56*, 603–616.

Lingard, L., & Haber, R. J. (1999). Teaching and learning communication in medicine: A rhetorical approach. *Academic Medicine, 74*, 507–510.

Lucas, K. (2016, January 3). Toward better business communication: Students at the University of Louisville learn to master five essential competencies of business communication. *BizEd*. Retrieved from https://bized.aacsb.edu

Martin, K. N., & Gaffney, A. L. H. (2016). Telling and showing: The intersection of visual communication content knowledge and pedagogical strategies in STEM. *Visual Communication Quarterly, 23*(2), 119–132.

Miles, M. B., & Huberman, A. M. (1984). *Qualitative data analysis: A sourcebook of new methods*. Beverly Hills, CA: Sage Publications.

Morton, J., & O'Brien, D. (2005). Selling your design: Oral communication pedagogy in design education. *Communication Education, 54*, 6–19.

Nathans-Kelly, T. M., & Evans, R. (2017). Creating Communicative Self-Efficacy Through Integrating and Innovating Engineering Communication Instruction. *ASEE* 2017. Columbus, OH.

National Academies of Sciences, Engineering, and Medicine. (2018). *The integration of the humanities and arts with sciences, engineering, and medicine in higher education: Branches from the same tree*. Washington, DC: The National Academies Press. doi:10.17226/24988

National Research Council. (2013). *Optics and photonics: Essential technologies for our nation*. Washington, DC: The National Academies Press. doi:10.17226/13491

Patton, M. Q. (1980). *Qualitative evaluation methods*. Beverly Hills, CA: Sage Publications.

Patton, M. Q. (1990). *Qualitative evaluation and research method*. Newbury Park, CA: Sage Publications.

Pellegrino, J. W., & Hilton, M. L. (Eds.). (2012). *Education for life and work: Developing transferable knowledge and skills in the 21st century*. Washington, DC: National Academies Press.

Saks, A. M., & Gruman, J. A. (2018). Socialization resources theory and newcomers' work engagement. *Career Development International, 23*(1), 12–32. doi:10.1108/cdi-12-2016-0214

Saks, A. M., Uggerslev, K. L., & Fassina, N. E. (2007). Socialization tactics and newcomer adjustment: A meta-analytic review and test of a model. *Journal of Vocational Behavior, 70*, 413–446. doi:10.1016/j.jvb.2006.12.004

Schaufeli, W. B., & Bakker, A. B. (2010). Defining and measuring work engagement: Bringing clarity to the concept. In A. B. Bakker, & M. P. Leiter (Eds.), *Work engagement: A handbook of essential theory and research* (pp. 10–24). New York, NY: Psychology Press.

Schaufeli, W. B., Salanova, M., Gonzalez-Roma, V., & Bakker, A. B. (2002). The measurement of engagement and burnout: A two sample confirmatory factor analytic approach. *Journal of Happiness Studies, 3*(1), 71–92.

Smith, E. (2005). Learning to talk like a teacher: Participation and negotiation in co-planning discourse. *Communication Education, 54*, 52–71.

Spradley, J. P. (1979). *The ethnographic interview*. New York: Holt, Rinehart and Winston.

Strauss, A. L., & Corbin, J. (1994). Grounded theory methodology: An overview. In N. K. Denzin, & Y. S. Lincoln (Eds.), *Handbook of qualitative research* (pp. 273–285). Thousand Oaks, CA: Sage.

Test, J. (2015, August 19). *American Institute for Manufacturing Integrated Photonics established in Rochester, New York*. Retrieved from https://www.rpcphotonics.com/american-institute-for-manufacturing-integrated-photonics-established-in-rochester-new-york/

Tryggvason, G., Thouless, M., Dutta, D., Ceccio, S. L., & Tilbury, D. M. (2001). The new mechanical engineering curriculum at the University of Michigan. *Journal of Engineering Education, 90*, 437–448.

Van Maanen, J., & Schein, E. H. (1979). Toward a theory of organizational socialization (B. M. Staw, Ed.). *Research in Organizational Behavior, 1*, 209–264.

Vrchota, D. (2011). Communication in the disciplines: Interpersonal communication in dietetics. *Communication Education, 60*, 210–230.

Wang, K. (2015). *Study on the careers of MIT mechanical engineering undergraduate alumni* (Unpublished master's thesis). Massachusetts Institute of Technology. Retrieved from http://hdl.handle.net/1721.1/98755

Appendix

Excerpts from Interview Protocol: Managers

General skills

1. When you have a new position available, how do you create the job descriptions?
2. Where do you post job descriptions? How do you find people who may be good candidates?
3. How do you decide who should be moved forward in the application process or be interviewed?
4. What skills do you think are most important for success in your company/research group?
5. For each of those skills, do you expect new employees to have it coming in? To develop it?
6. How are you defining success? Doing well in a particular entry-level position? Moving up in the company?
7. Do you see a lot of unqualified applicants?
   a. If yes, what fraction?
   b. What are the most common deficiencies you see in applicants?
8. Does your institution/organization support continuing education or on-the-job training?
9. What are the differences between an Associates and a BS-level position in terms of job description?
   a. What are the differences in terms of key skills expected coming in?
   b. Are associates-level positions ever promotable to higher skill jobs?
   c. If so, does that happen through internal training or do employees go back to school?
10. How important is cultural "fit" or similarity between the applicant and the culture of the company/university in the hiring process? How do you best determine "fit"?

Communication competence

1. What communication tasks/situations (e.g., making presentations to clients, writing internal reports, summarizing research) do employees take part in in daily/weekly (routine tasks) or as needed (difficult/important tasks)?
2. What tools (e.g., PowerPoint, whiteboards) do these tasks involve?
3. Which of these types of tasks do you expect employees to have experienced prior to employmentWhich do employees experience after employment ?
4. What communication competencies (e.g., writing, speaking, listening, interpersonal) are employees expected to use on the job?
   a. Do you notice any trends in the communication strengths or weaknesses of new hires? What are the trends?
5. What training opportunities, if any, exist to help employees develop communication skills on the job?

Skills gap

1. When degrees in science, engineering, and technology are connected with workforce issues, it is often claimed there is a "skills gap." Are you familiar with this term "skills gap"?
2. If so, how would you define it? What do you think is typically meant?
3. Are there any skills that are unique to your particular company/research position?
   a. What particular skills would you say are essential prior to hire vs. skills they can learn on the job?
   b. Are there any intangible skills (leadership, adaptability, multitasking, etc.) you think are especially relevant for these kinds of positions?

4. Do you have any advice for students preparing for employment?
5. Do you have any advice for the academic programs and faculty preparing students for employment?
6. If there are holes in training or knowledge of a new employee, how is that viewed and handled? How is training then provided?

Teaching advocacy communication to pediatric residents: the efficacy of applied improvisational theater (AIT) as an instructional tool

Krista Hoffmann-Longtin, Jason M. Organ, Jill V. Helphinstine, Deanna R. Reinoso, Zachary S. Morgan and Elizabeth Weinstein

ABSTRACT
In today's communication landscape, the public often turn to the Internet and social media instead of their physician for health information. To remain relevant and respected amidst the wealth of health information available online, physicians need to offer something the Internet cannot fully emulate: empathetic imagination and an ability to instantaneously tailor messages to reach and teach worried and often confused audiences effectively. We developed an instructional communication module for pediatric residents that used applied improvisational theater to help residents develop complex and dynamic communication skills. The module included opportunities to develop empathy, practice audience analysis, distill messages to key points, and apply these skills in media and community contexts. Attendees completed surveys regarding their perceptions of curricular structure, efficacy, and utility. Preliminary results indicate gains in communication confidence and skills. This type of instructional communication and training module encourages healthcare practitioners to position themselves as trusted experts and partners in helping clients make meaning of health information, thus empowering a new generation of pediatricians to bridge communication gaps created by new technologies and increased access to multiple information sources.

Physicians today must do more than heal; they must also teach patients to navigate an ever-growing sea of online medical information with a discerning and analytical eye (Funk, 2017; Konnikova, 2014). The challenge for physicians is this: when the public go to the Internet for information and advice regarding health and wellness, they often leave confused or misinformed; not knowing what or who to trust. This cultural phenomenon—googling symptoms, diagnoses, and even remedies for anything from the common cold to more serious diseases—has created a crisis in the health professions community, perhaps most notably seen with the antivaccination movement (Funk, 2017), which has compelled many to disregard scientific evidence. This movement and others have led many in the health community to think about communication with the public differently than in the past. In fact, a recent editorial in the *New England Journal of Medicine* posed the question, "How do we convince a skeptical public to believe in science?" (Rosenbaum, 2017, p. 1607). Whereas many physicians are trained in empathetic communication and medical expertise, most are not taught the kind of trust-building communication skills required to help patients manage these types of conflicting health messages (Lee & Hornik, 2009). The bottom line is that shifts in society's relationship with medical information means that doctors must learn a new set of communication skills.

As a subset of the general physician population, pediatricians are in a particularly important position when communicating with the general public. In 2005, former U.S. Surgeon General David Satcher and colleagues argued that it is the responsibility of pediatricians to advocate for children's health both in the exam room and the public sphere, as children are unable to advocate for themselves (Satcher, Kaczorowski, & Topa, 2005). Given the importance of this advocacy work, the Accreditation Council for Graduate Medical Education (ACGME) began requiring that pediatric residency programs include elements of advocacy and community-based pediatrics. Specifically, residents must demonstrate proficiency in communicating "effectively with patients, families and the public, as appropriate, across a broad range of socioeconomic and cultural backgrounds" (ACGME, 2017, p. 16). Historically, formal instruction for pediatric residents on advocacy-related communication skills has been limited to lectures, field trips to learn more about community resources, and tool boxes, with the expectation that residents will learn to advocate in the same way that they learn clinical skills: "see one, do one, teach one" (Lichtenstein, Hoffman, & Moon, 2017). These types of lectures and toolboxes may arm pediatric residents with necessary content expertise, but they may also leave them deficient in the actual development of the advocacy-related communication skills required to address the public's current lack of trust in medicine, particularly related to children's and adolescents' health.

This study explores a novel programmatic instructional intervention designed to teach pediatric residents how to communicate effectively in advocacy settings, whether with news media or the community. Our program used applied improvisational theater (AIT), a theoretically based pedagogical approach that has become popular for teaching communication to health professionals (Hoffmann-Longtin, Rossing, & Weinstein, 2018; Kaplan-Liss et al., 2018; Sawyer, Fu, Gray, & Umoren, 2017; Watson, 2011). Specifically, we designed our day-long instructional intervention with the aim of helping pediatric residents become more comfortable and confident advocating for children's health issues. Ultimately, instructional programs like this one could be important tools to help pediatricians counteract misinformation proliferated in today's Internet and social media landscape.

In this article, we first define physician advocacy and advocacy communication, particularly in the context of pediatrics. We follow with the theoretical grounding for using AIT in our instructional intervention program. Then, we discuss the landscape for communication instruction in healthcare settings, generally, and AIT specifically, and propose our research questions. We then describe our methodology and results. Finally, we conclude with a discussion about how this study fits into the larger conversation regarding effective communication instruction for healthcare professionals.

Health advocacy definitions and frameworks

Although debates exist about how to define health advocacy, one often cited definition suggests that it involves "action by a physician to promote those social, economic, educational, and political changes that ameliorate the suffering and threats to human health and well-being that he or she identifies through his or her professional work and expertise" (Earnest, Wong, & Federico, 2010, p. 63). Calls for health advocacy training have been widespread (Earnest et al., 2010; Frenk et al., 2010; Gruen, Campbell, & Blumenthal, 2006; Kanter, 2011; Shipley et al., 2005), arguing generally for medical students "to develop skills in advocacy theory, execution, and communication" (Dworkis, Wilbur, & Sandel, 2010, p. 1549). Health advocacy skill development is also critical in the pediatric subfield. For example, in their 2005 call for pediatric health advocacy, Satcher and colleagues argued that—because so much of pediatric health is determined by social and community factors—it is pediatricians' responsibility to improve the health and well-being of their communities through advocacy efforts. As Satcher et al. (2005) explain, "to improve child health, physicians must work within their communities to identify the needs of the population they serve and take appropriate action to influence the needs of private and public policies that address these needs" (p. 1124). Heeding this call, in 2009, the Pediatrics Residency Review Committee began requiring advocacy training and experience for all pediatric resident physicians in the U.S. (Earnest et al., 2010). Yet how to best teach medical students and pediatric residents to advocate effectively has been the topic of much debate in medical education (Dworkis et al., 2010; Hubinette, Dobson, Scott, & Sherbino, 2017; Kanter, 2011; Martin & Whitehead, 2013). Debates arise from differing definitions of what counts as advocacy and who counts as the expert in an advocacy setting. Whereas Earnest and colleagues' (2010) definition locates the responsibility for advocacy (and the expertise) with the physician, other scholars locate expertise and advocacy efforts in more of a communal setting. Moreover, Brown et al. (2004) differentiate between health advocacy and activism, arguing that advocates tend to work within the current systemic structure, whereas health activists challenge the traditional structure by insisting on lay participation in knowledge production. Specifically, Zoller (2005) suggests that studying the communicative behaviors of health advocacy and activities has been problematic, since most research focuses on activism associated with a particular disease state (such as HIV/AIDS activism or breast cancer activism) rather than as a set of discursive practices used by community activist groups in general.

Debates aside, it is clear that issues related to advocacy and activism are complex. Hubinette et al. (2017) proposed a theoretical framework for advocacy in medicine that captures many of these complexities. The authors describe two axes of advocacy work: vertical and horizontal. The vertical axis represents the types of and levels at which advocacy occurs, from individual (developing individual agency by navigating through and removing barriers in the healthcare system) to institutional (engaging in activism activities designed to bring about system-level changes that persist once the efforts of the advocate have ended). Agency activities include providing information to and educating patients, connecting patients with community resources, referring patients to nonclinical professionals, and navigating health or other systems that would difficult for the patient to navigate independently (e.g., supportive housing systems). Participation in these types of advocacy efforts affords health advocates an opportunity to act as an agent working within the constraints of the system on behalf of the patient. On the other pole of the vertical axis is activism, which is designed to alter the system (i.e., results in institutional, social, economic, or political change). Activist behaviors do not simply operate within the bounds of the system as agency activities do. They focus on changing the system, structurally. Examples of activism strategies include raising awareness of problematic issues on behalf of patients, or advocating for social, political, or economic changes in the system.

The horizontal axis of Hubinette et al.'s (2017) theoretical framework represents who determines the need for advocacy: a shared group of experts and community members or one expert (without the collaboration with the community). With shared approaches to advocacy, priorities are determined collaboratively among the patient, the clinician, and the community. Shared approaches to advocacy require that the clinician position their biomedical expertise alongside (and not above) the knowledge, experiences, and desires of the patient and community. Shared advocacy could involve a physician serving on a community board or advocating in the news media in partnership with a community group. Such shared approaches are contrasted with directed advocacy activities, where an individual clinician provides perspective, expertise, and guidance on an issue; speaking for (not with) an individual patient or community. Directed advocacy activities could include calling a clinical specialist to get an urgent investigation for a patient, making sure that patients have required health information, or offering referrals to community agencies and organizations. As Hubinette et al. (2017) argue, in order to equip future healthcare professionals to reduce health inequities, we must equip them with communication skills to lead and advocate; the axes allow professionals to locate themselves strategically and intentionally within various advocacy roles. Although the model provides an important starting point for health professionals, it does not provide insight into the communication aspects of these advocacy roles. Pearce and Cronen's (1980) coordinated management of meaning offers one potential approach.

Coordinated management of meaning and health advocacy

The complex nature of health advocacy settings and the potential tensions involved with the varied participants and contexts (e.g., physicians, patients, the public; online, face-to-face, mediated) make it important to understand how meanings are negotiated and instantiated within these settings. Coordinated management of meaning (CMM) (Pearce, 1989, 2004, 2007; Pearce & Cronen, 1980) provides a useful theoretical framework. According to Pearce and Cronen (1980), perceiving messages is not the challenging part of communication. Rather, we struggle to communicate effectively because we are constantly managing the meaning of our communication as a way to coherently tell the stories of our experiences. We always manage these meanings in the context of others, thus coordinating the meaning with them (Pearce, 2004; Pearce & Cronen, 1980) and creating the social worlds within which messages are understood and interpreted. Although advocacy is, by nature, persuasive, a CMM lens would suggest that advocacy be considered as a process of developing partnerships and coordinating meaning, rather than simply focusing on convincing an audience to believe a particular message.

CMM proposes two types of rules that govern conversation: constitutive (rules that help to determine what is appropriate in a given context and how to interpret the meaning of an event or message) and regulative (rules that govern action or next steps in a conversation).

Both constitutive and regulative rules are always enacted by communicators based on a context. For example, the constitutive rules of discussing vaccine hesitancy are different in a news interview than patient room. In both cases, the topic should be approached with empathy and a focus on acknowledging emotions rather just sharing facts. However, it may be more appropriate for a physician to focus on distilling the message to a few key points in a television interview, and alternatively, the patient room might warrant more of a focus on asking questions to seek understanding. Recognizing the contexts of the television interview and the patient room, and the varied advocacy strategies related to those distinct contexts and conversations, is important so that the physician can best reach the intended audiences.

Two more key concepts of CMM are useful as they relate to advocacy in healthcare settings: coherence (the stories participants use to make meaning within the conversations) and coordination (the extent to which two communicators agree upon the pattern or story they are creating together, within the conversation). For example, a pediatrician does not have to agree with a parent's hesitancy to vaccinate (they might not necessarily share the same story about vaccines); however, that physician must accept that the parent's fears are part of the story and meaning they are ascribing to the interaction. To move forward, the physician and parent need to coordinate their narratives; working together to decide where the hesitancy comes from and what to do about it. The extent to which this happens can largely influence the effectiveness of the advocacy efforts.

The CMM approach can be helpful in public advocacy settings, in addition to conversations at the bedside. Because they are trained as scientists, physicians' default approach to advocacy is often to share more information about a topic in order to persuade an audience based on evidence. Yet often the public are acting emotionally, on a basis of fear, when issues of health are in question. For example, as related to the antivaccine movement, parents have likely heard stories or seen a social media video about the (inaccurate) relationship between autism and vaccines, creating anxiety and uncertainty. A CMM lens might suggest a physician approach a television interview by acknowledging the social media stories that are compelling to many parents; then focusing the message on the common values shared by parents and physicians—keeping children safe and healthy (thus attending to the emotions and fears parents could be feeling). After discussing this shared goal, the physician might share an anecdote of a patient who was helped by a vaccine, as well as data and information. Thus, the physician is attending to both the coherence (acknowledging the stories that contribute to parents' fears) and coordination (emphasizing shared values/commitments to children's health) and of the message with the audience.

This study uses a CMM lens, along with Hubinette et al.'s (2017) advocacy framework, to understand the complexities of communicating in health advocacy settings (and in particular, pediatric health advocacy settings). Given the myriad of health messages (of varying degrees of accuracy) that patients and families have access to, it is critical to teach future pediatricians to advocate effectively by navigating carefully between fact and fear and coordinating messages appropriately. It is no longer about simply delivering information. Rather, as CMM theory suggests, physicians (in order to be effective advocates) must work to create shared meaning in partnership with patients. Doing this may be challenging for physicians who have been trained to focus on data and information, rather than on building empathy to coordinate information with patients and the public. Since health advocacy has become more complex with the wealth of information available to the general public, there are multiple approaches and contexts in which physicians must advocate to improve the system of care and, ultimately, the health of their patients. These complexities merit attention, particularly as they inform instructional training programs for physicians.

Communication instruction in health contexts

Communication instruction in medicine (Makoul, 2001), nursing, and the veterinary fields is a cornerstone of the professional education process. In medical education specifically, communication instruction (often called communication skills training or CST) has primarily focused on one-on-one patient–provider communication at the bedside (Brown et al., 2010; Brown & Bylund, 2008; Cegala & Lenzmeier Broz, 2002; Donovan, Love, Mackert, Vangelisti, & Ring, 2017; Gysels, Richardson, & Higginson, 2004). The focus stands to reason, as it is in the context of the patient–provider relationship that diagnosis and treatment occurs. As Donovan and colleagues (2017) explain, "[i]mportant goals of communication training are enhancing providers' ability to build rapport, empathize, gather data, and explain complex information, all of which need to be understood as building blocks of communication knowledge" (p. 491). While many healthcare practitioners are trained in building empathy and trust at the bedside, the techniques best suited to teach these skills are understudied, in particular as they are related to advocacy efforts (Brown & Bylund, 2008; Donovan et al., 2017).

Cegala and Lenzmeier Broz (2002) conducted a literature review of studies focusing on CST. Reviewing studies published between 1990 and 2002, the authors closely examined 26 studies focused on the objectives and communication skills taught in communication education programs in health fields. Their results suggest that research on CST is varied: trainings ranged in length from one hour to five days and included multiple types of pre/post-tests and feedback mechanisms. Most importantly, trainings rarely specified an instructional focus on particular communication skills. Despite this, the authors concluded that CST can be used to effectively alter participants' behavior in patient encounters. However, they did suggest that researchers should be much more specific about the communication skills being taught and evaluated, and that those skills should be grounded in a theoretical framework. Brown and Bylund (2008) later replicated this meta-analysis: in the 18 additional studies they found, they concluded that, although there was more alignment between objectives and assessment, trainings still failed to specifically identify concrete and measurable communication skills. To that end, Brown and Bylund (2008) developed the Comskil conceptual model, which defines the central communication components of a patient–provider encounter and strategies for teaching and assessing those skills. Their model differentiates and offers definitions for communication goals (what a communicator hopes to accomplish), strategies (what plans direct communication toward a goal), and skills (the unit of speech a speaker uses to achieve a goal). This model provides a more systematic approach to program design and allows curriculum designers to create teaching strategies and assessments which are grounded in particular communication needs of the health care setting. Although these analyses suggest CST is happening, both illustrate the need for more specific identification and rigorous evaluation of the CST themselves, leading to a better understanding of the most effective way to teach dynamic communication skills in healthcare settings generally and as related to healthcare advocacy specifically.

AIT

Although studies have called for the identification of concrete measurable communication skills in CST, recent scholars have also acknowledged that training focusing exclusively on learning these skills in a checklist manner limits physicians' abilities related to communicative flexibility: being able to adapt their communication in the moment for a variety of audiences and contexts (Egener & Cole-Kelly, 2004; Eisenberg, Rosenthal, & Schlussel, 2015; Kaplan-Liss et al., 2018; Salmon & Young, 2011; Zoppi & Epstein, 2002). For example, Levinson, Lesser, and Epstein (2010) contend that building effective relationships in healthcare "cannot be accomplished by mechanically applying skills. Rather they require genuine personal engagement and emotional involvement" (p. 1311). How to teach communicative flexibility has been the subject of a significant body of scholarship, as well (e.g., Deveugele et al., 2005; Kurtz, Draper, & Silverman, 2004; Makoul & Schofield, 1999; Rider & Keefer, 2006). Some health education programs use experiential education methods (such as role play and simulation) (Cegala & Lenzmeier Broz, 2002; Gysels et al., 2004) and specifically, programs have turned to the techniques of improvisational theater (often called AIT) to train physicians to speak and write more spontaneously, flexibly, responsively, and engagingly to a variety of audiences (Hoffmann-Longtin et al., 2018; Kaplan-Liss et al., 2018; Sawyer et al., 2017; Watson, 2011). As a theoretical lens and pedagogical practice, "[t]he field of AIT translates the theory, practice, and training strategies of the theater into real-world contexts on the basis that the communication skills and the habits of thinking and acting that make a successful improviser on stage are the same skills and habits that foster success in other contexts" (Hoffmann-Longtin, Rossing, & Donovan, 2018, p. 5). Instructional training models using AIT encourage participants to see communication as a participatory partnership between physicians and patients (within and outside of the patient room) and encourage a close analysis of the audience to develop and coordinate culturally competent and dynamic messages. Results of these AIT instructional programs have been promising. For example, Berk and Trieber (2009) suggest that improvisation allows learners to grow through experiential discovery and collaboration, which in turn promotes deeper learning. Additionally, these techniques have demonstrated themselves to be effective in teaching communication flexibility in other disciplines, such as nursing (Hanley & Fenton, 2007), pharmacy (Boesen, Herrier, Apgar, & Jackowski, 2009), business (Scinto, 2014), and education (Rossing & Hoffmann-Longtin, 2016; Sawyer, 2011).

AIT uses experiential exercises, sometimes called drills, to engage participants in practicing the habits necessary to accomplish learning goals. Rather than memorizing a list of communication behaviors, these drills ask participants to try out approaches to communication in their own words in a supportive environment. Following each drill is a period of debrief where participants are asked to reflect on the affective and social benefits of these approaches. In doing so, facilitators connect the participants' observations to extant communication theory, making explicit not just what behaviors work, but *why* they work in a particular interaction or context. A series of tenets or principles underscore the AIT pedagogy. In improvisational theater, these are often called rules. A short summary of these principles follows (for more detail, see Berk & Trieber, 2009; Hoffmann-Longtin et al., 2018; Hoffmann-Longtin et al., 2018; Jagodowski & Pasquesi, 2015; Rossing & Hoffmann-Longtin, 2016).

- *Yes, and ...* It is a communicator's goal to accept the reality of our conversational partner and keep the conversation moving forward.
- *Make your scene partner look good,* or *take care of your partner.* It is a communicator's responsibility to take care of and support their conversational partner by taking an other-oriented or audience-centered approach to their communication.
- *Follow the follower.* Communicators should look to their conversational partner for direction on how they should approach a topic. They should listen closely, without judgement, asking questions to determine next steps.
- *There are no mistakes,* or *everything is a gift.* Communicators should accept mistakes or missteps as opportunities to learn more about their conversational partner's perspective and to build empathy and trust.

Grounded in Hubinette et al.'s (2017) advocacy framework for understanding the ways in which physicians coordinate meanings with patients and the public, and using the Comskil training instructional design approach (Brown et al., 2010; Brown & Bylund, 2008), we developed our AIT pilot curriculum to teach advocacy-related communication skills to pediatric residents during their community advocacy rotation. By using the AIT pedagogy, we sought to problematize residents' current definition of communication as simply bi-directional message exchange. Rather, we hoped our residents would consider the roles of audience analysis, message design, and cocreation of meaning as an important part of their advocacy responsibility. This seven-hour interactive curriculum was embedded as a one-day workshop into an already-existing month-long community advocacy rotation. The advocacy rotation is an ideal setting for this instructional program because residents are asked to move beyond bedside communication to consult in community educational settings and create a podcast for a community partner on a health topic of importance to their constituents. We hypothesized that, after completion of this workshop and rotation, residents would feel more prepared to participate in advocacy activities, such as speaking to the media and community partners, as compared with their baseline readiness. Four research questions (RQs) guided our mixed methods approach to evaluating the AIT curriculum and subsequent changes in our participants:

RQ1: How did residents' perceptions of their willingness and ability to advocate (both in the community and in the media) change after participating in the AIT workshop?

RQ2: What advocacy-related communication techniques (taught during the workshop) became sustained practices for residents over time?

RQ3: What did residents perceive as ongoing barriers to advocacy communication following the workshop?

RQ4: What did residents perceive as effective and ineffective advocacy strategies (from the workshop) in their workplace settings?

Methods

To answer our four RQs, we collected quantitative and qualitative data, immediately pre-/postintervention, as well as in a follow-up survey a few months after the intervention. Prior to discussing the methodology in detail, we provide a summary of the AIT training curriculum, as it was the setting within which we collected data from pediatric residents.

Setting: AIT curriculum in pediatric advocacy rotations

We developed and delivered our AIT instructional workshop to a total of 51 residents. The audience for each workshop included five to 12 resident participants. The workshop was conducted in the context of the month-long pediatric community advocacy rotation. There were nine month-long rotations over the period of a year, within each of which we held one day-long workshop. The rotation included on-site observations and partnerships with community organizations to produce health messaging events and materials such as community meetings, pamphlets, and podcasts. All residents on the rotation were expected to attend the workshop prior to completing their rotation.

The overall goal of the workshop focused on using policy information and empathetic message design to build trust in the field of medicine, to better advocate, and to correct misinformation. Specifically, we focused on our residents' dynamic responsiveness, empathetic connection, and audience-centeredness in their communication. In order to acknowledge the complexities involved with advocacy in pediatric–patient–community relationships, we offered the ACGME (2017) definition of advocacy while at the same time providing opportunities to discuss the notion of lay expertise and power imbalances in the context of communicating about health issues for systemic change (Earnest et al., 2010; Hubinette et al., 2017).

Learning outcomes for the workshop focused on residents' abilities to (1) explain the importance of clear communication and recognize how to create clear meanings with different audiences; (2) attend to the needs of an audience, read verbal and nonverbal cues, and adjust communication in the moment, as needed; (3) reduce self-consciousness in communication; and (4) use storytelling techniques effectively to evoke emotion, build empathy, and make personal connections through clear, vivid language. In developing the curriculum, we worked with the rotation faculty to understand the communication needs and challenges faced by their trainees and colleagues (Brown et al., 2010).

Our workshop consisted of four sections: (1) Improvisation for Physicians, (2) Distilling Your Message, (3) Partnering with the Community, and (4) Media Training. Each section was approximately 90 min, with short breaks in between. Each section included 1–3 AIT drills, with a semistructured debriefing period immediately following. Drills were chosen based on established research on AIT in medical education (Hoffmann-Longtin et al., 2018; Kaplan-Liss et al., 2018; Sawyer et al., 2017; Watson, 2011). The following is a description of each section of the workshop, with an example of the drills used and the communication goals for each.

Session 1: improvisation for scientists

The first session was designed to introduce the participants to AIT as a training strategy for advocacy communication. The exercises were chosen to help the residents speak about their work effectively and responsively with multiple audiences, from peers and professors to family members and policymakers. During the exercises, residents practiced connecting with an audience, paying attention to others, reading nonverbal cues, and responding freely without self-consciousness. For example, in one drill called *Mirror*, participants were asked (in pairs) to move their bodies nonverbally, serving as a mirror to each other (Kaplan-Liss et al., 2018). When person A began to move, person B would try to mirror person A's movements. Success was defined as near-perfect mirroring, such that an observer would not know who was leading and who was following. This game encouraged participants to focus exclusively on their audience, making continuous adjustments to ensure that their audience was following their communication. Consistent with AIT pedagogy, participants were side coached while participating in the activity (Hoffmann-Longtin et al., 2018). Facilitators encouraged participants to take care of their partners (a principle of AIT), illustrating the co-construction of meaning that occurs in communication settings. In another activity called *Photograph*, learners were asked to describe a meaningful photograph from their lives using a blank white sheet of paper as their canvas (Hoffmann-Longtin et al., 2018). This exercise encouraged participants to use rich descriptive language and analogy, such that the audience could imagine the actual portrait. Debriefing included a conversation about the extent to which the audience remembered the emotional or relational message more saliently than the content of the message (Watzlawick, Beavin, & Jackson, 1967). These exercises helped residents to be audience-centered and to build clarity and engagement through verbal and nonverbal communication. Further, it oriented them to the importance of ensuring that their audiences were following their messages in a way that promoted understanding and connection.

Session 2: distilling your message

Session 2 introduced principles of clear communication and featured AIT drills through which residents practiced speaking clearly and vividly about science in ways lay audiences could understand and appreciate. The participants practiced crafting a short, clear, engaging statements about their work and why it matters. While doing so, the session addressed how to communicate at different levels of complexity to different audiences. Learners practiced defining their communication goals, identifying main points, explaining meaning and context, responding to questions, and using storytelling techniques to enliven messages. In the cornerstone exercise for this session, participants utilized short policy statements from the American Academy of Pediatrics (AAP) on important advocacy topics (such as car seat use, smoking cessation, and vaccination) as catalysts for conversation (AAP, 2018). In an activity entitled *Half Life*, participants worked in pairs to take turns distilling their chosen advocacy topic into increasingly shorter time periods, from 2 min to 1 min to 30 s and then finally to 15 s. Afterwards, each speaker interviewed their partner, asking them to identify the main point of their message, the most memorable parts of the message, as well as what the message makes the listener want to do. This process compelled the communicator to clearly define their goal in short, accessible terms; teaching them to add vivid detail and description as time and audience interest allows.

Session 3: partnering with the community

This session focused on equipping learners with techniques for shared meaning-making and collaboration with community partners. These methods have been shown to be particularly useful in health advocacy because, as Hubinette and colleagues' (2017) explain, they level the playing field between experts and community members, acknowledging the expertise that patients bring to any interaction. Activities focused on developing trust, opening lines of communication, and sharing expertise in a way that values and respects the lived experiences of community members. Many of the exercises focused on finding areas of connection, rather than disagreement, with patients and community members. During the final exercise of this session, learners were invited to repeat a version of the "photograph" exercise from session 1, this time painting a picture of a meaningful patient encounter and how this story might be told in an advocacy context. This exercise focused on helping learners to connect the tenets of effective storytelling with the goal of advocacy.

Session 4: media training
The final session of the day was designed to build confidence and efficacy in speaking in one advocacy setting: a public interview with a journalist about the advocacy topic identified during the "Distilling Your Message" session. The following scenario was provided to the residents:

> You have been invited to a local parent–teacher meeting to participate in a public interview based on the topic you chose earlier from the AAP policy statement. During your short interview, you will be asked to speak authoritatively and engagingly on this topic. Local media will be there, so you expect that a few sound bites from your interview might be used on the evening news.

Each participant was given 5–10 min to prepare, and then the interview was conducted with a journalist in front of the workshop participants. After each interview, the participant was asked to reflect on what they thought they did especially well, and what they would do differently if they were interviewed again. Additional feedback was solicited from the workshop participants. While traditional AIT techniques were not included in this session, facilitators consistently employed debriefing techniques informed by AIT to maintain the tone of the workshop. For example, after the interview, those workshop participants who observed the interview are asked what they would add to the interview. By focusing feedback on extending the conversation, rather than what went wrong, the facilitators reinforce the AIT principle of Yes, and …

Participants

Fifty one pediatric residents participated in the training program. Resident physicians are those trainees who have completed medical school and are now completing an additional 3–7 years of training in the specialty field of their choice. This training (called residency) comprises a set of specific rotations designed to expose physicians to critical areas in their specialty.

During residency, residents complete rotations to learn to care for patients with varied needs. For example, in pediatrics, rotations might include caring for critically ill and premature newborns, children with lung disease, and children with cancer. Rotations may vary in length but are usually 4 weeks long. Some rotations are embedded longitudinally throughout training, and many rotations are repeated multiple times during residency training. Community advocacy is a rotation that is required by the accrediting body for pediatric residents (ACGME, 2017). At our institution, the community advocacy rotation occurs in years 1 and 2 of the pediatric residency program. We imbedded our workshop within this month-long rotation.

Of our resident participants in the workshop, 65% were women. This overrepresentation of women mirrors the field of pediatrics, where approximately 62% of the population are women (Association of American Medical Colleges, 2015). Due to the relatively small sample size, race and ethnic data about the participants were not collected to protect their anonymity.

Data collection and analysis

Two sources of quantitative data were used to evaluate the effectiveness of the AIT workshop: a pre-/postsurvey and a follow-up survey. The pre- and postsurveys asked identical questions and were developed and employed previously by the course directors for the community advocacy rotation.[1] These surveys were distributed to all 51 residents who participated in the workshop. The questions primarily asked about willingness to engage with the media to discuss health topics, as well as the extent to which the residents felt the media influenced their patients' health practices and beliefs. All questions used a 5-point Likert scale, except for one question that used a 4-point scale (not at all difficult to very difficult). We maintained the same survey, despite the inconsistency in the Likert scale, for comparison between the groups before and after the workshop intervention. Survey questions[2] asked to what extent the participants thought media influenced their patients' health practices and beliefs, as well as to what extent they were willing to engage in advocacy activities in the media (such as participating in interviews or writing magazine articles). To measure the program's effectiveness, independent sample t-tests examined the difference in means between the surveys completed before the workshop and those completed after the workshop.

The second set of data involved a follow-up survey[2] sent to the participants between 6 and 12 months after they had participated in the workshop. This follow-up survey asked to what extent, as a result of participating in the program, the residents used communication techniques such as listening to their audience, using rich descriptions and storytelling, and building trust through voice and body language. These items also used a 5-point Likert scale. As there was no presurvey for these data, we report resident responses using simple descriptive statistics. To provide a richer description of the participants' experience, we also asked several open-ended qualitative questions on the follow-up survey, including those that asked participants to define effective and ineffective communication.

Responses to the qualitative survey items were analyzed for emergent themes. Consistent with the trustworthiness strategies established by Lincoln and Guba (1985), each member of the research team read the written answers to each open-ended question at least twice and discussed the meaning of the response in the context of the RQs and the other responses. Then, the research team used an inductive process to identify emergent themes across multiple responses. Separate elements were placed into larger categories, and the research team developed thematic descriptors to represent the sentiment of each section or cluster (Patton, 2002). We analyzed the relationships among the clusters, referring to process notes to confirm themes, and developed higher-level themes that connected several related concepts (Patton, 2002). After returning to the original data, representative examples of each theme were identified from the surveys. To ensure a rigorous analytical process, colleagues not involved in the research (but familiar with the program) served as peer debriefers (Lincoln & Guba, 1985), asking questions and helping the research team to clarify themes and categories.

Results

Of the 51 residents who participated in the workshop, 37 completed the presurvey and 34 completed the postsurvey, indicating response rates of 72% and 67% respectively. Twenty-five of the 51 residents completed the follow-up survey—a 49% response rate. Results of the pre- and postsurvey and the follow-up survey, including the qualitative response thematic analysis, are combined and discussed together with consideration to our central RQs. Representative quotations from each theme are included, and participants were assigned pseudonyms to protect their anonymity.

RQ1: perceptions of willingness and ability to advocate in media and community

Residents reported that their willingness to engage in advocacy communication with community members, policymakers, and the media to discuss health topics significantly increased following the workshop, as shown in Table 1. Also, residents felt much better qualified to give an interview or otherwise participate in the media on health topics as a result of participating in our workshop (mean increase from 2.73 to 3.43). (Other responses in Table 1 were not significant after Bonferroni correction.) The table also shows that participants found writing and recording a health podcast to be less difficult after the workshop when compared with their responses prior to the workshop. In the follow-up survey, most participants agreed or strongly agreed that they continued to find additional resources to communicate healthcare issues more effectively. They also seem to agree that they continue to use the techniques of the workshop.

Open-ended questions in the follow-up survey suggested that participants saw themselves as being willing to advocate both in organization-based advocacy and individual-based advocacy, and a few saw this work as occurring in the media. For example, some residents mentioned their participation in professional organizations as an important part of their advocacy communication. Katherine mentioned her role on a hospital-based patient safety advocacy committee, and Lyle mentioned joining the local AAP chapter. More frequently, our participants remarked on their individual participation in advocacy. Phoebe explained, "I had the ability to contact my state senator regarding topics that I have felt strongly about." Similarly, Trisha said she had been "calling and leaving voicemails related to the Children's Health Insurance Plan and healthcare funding with my representative." One participant, Gail, indicated that she continued to engage in the production of the podcast created within her advocacy rotation.

Table 1. Pre- and postsurvey summary.

	Presurvey mean (SD)	Postsurvey mean (SD)	Mean diff.	Sig.
If asked, I would be willing to discuss a health topic with a reporter on the evening news	3.08 (0.97)	3.55 (0.79)	0.46	0.03
If asked, I would be willing to do a telephone interview for a parenting magazine	3.30 (0.85)	3.70 (0.73)	0.40	0.04
If asked, I would be willing to make a written contribution to a magazine or newspaper article on a health topic	3.91 (0.51)	4.18 (0.52)	0.26	0.04
I feel qualified to give an interview or otherwise participate in the media on health topics	2.73 (0.83)	3.43 (0.78)	0.70	0.001*
How difficult do you think it is to write and record a health podcast?	2.86 (0.76)	2.39 (0.83)	−0.47	0.17

*Significance beyond the 0.01 threshold based on a Bonferroni adjustment of .05 for five analyses.

RQ2: sustained communication techniques

Residents indicated that they learned several communication techniques during the workshop that they continued to employ following the workshop. These techniques included (1) listening more closely to understand the needs of their patients, patient families, colleagues, and the community; (2) using rich descriptions and analogies to enhance empathy with their audience and to help their audience understand complicated information; (3) using storytelling as an effective way to communicate with an audience; (4) modifying communication plan based on the response of their audience; and (5) using voice and body language to create a sense of trust with the audience (Table 2).

Qualitative data also illustrate how residents sustained their communication practices in three areas: message distillation, empathy, and language transformation. Residents identified increased attention to making messages more succinct and understandable for nonexperts; a technique we call *distilling* in the workshop. This concept was mentioned frequently in the participants' comments. Ashley suggested: "I try to simplify my message and tailor my phrasing based upon the level of sophistication of the audience." Rachel also stated, "Leaving a voicemail related to children's health insurance funding, I think I used short, relatable information."

In addition to distilling, the participants also mentioned developing more empathetic messages after the training. This is best exemplified by Phoebe who stated, "I think I try to understand more where the other person is coming from and what their goals are." Trisha mentioned an exercise where they used vivid detail to describe their experience taking care of a patient that may be related to an advocacy issue. As she remarked, "Being able to describe my favorite patient that I've gotten to take care of. Always nice to have reminders that the more we connect with our patients, the more we fight for them." Finally, residents reported language transformation as a sustained communication practice. They articulated activities that involved describing a picture using vivid and rich detail, with the goal of translating that into their advocacy settings. Additionally, participants remarked that they continued to change language to better meet the needs of audiences. For example, Katherine said, "I sit down and explain in more understandable terms." Frances similarly explained, "I try to tailor my phrasing based upon the level of sophistication of the audience." Trisha echoed this, "I'm able to relate to [patients] using anecdotes and analogies better."

Table 2. Follow-up survey summary.

	Mean (SD)
I have identified additional resources to communicate about health care issues effectively	4.20 (0.65)
I use techniques from the Workshop to communicate about health care issues	4.16 (0.69)
I listen more closely to understand the needs of my audience (e.g., patients, families, colleagues, and the community)	4.28 (0.79)
I use rich descriptions and analogies to enhance empathy with my audience	4.12 (0.83)
I use rich descriptions and analogies to help the audience understand complicated information	4.16 (0.69)
I use storytelling to connect with my audience	4.08 (0.76)
I modify my communication plan based on the response of my audience	4.56 (0.58)
I use voice and body language to create a sense of trust in my audience	4.36 (0.57)
I feel more confident in my ability to listen to audience concerns	4.28 (0.61)
I feel more confident in my ability to reframe my message based on my audience's needs	4.44 (0.65)

RQ3: ongoing barriers to advocacy communication

In terms of ongoing barriers to communicating in advocacy settings (and in particular, with the media), several residents noted that they did not perceive any barriers. Those who did report barriers focused on lack of time, opportunity, and self-efficacy. Many respondents simply gave one-word answers to identify these barriers (e.g., "opportunity," "schedule," "knowledge"). Others provided more detail; for example, Rachel suggested, "Time, and I haven't really initiated any opportunities." For those who did provide more detail, a lack of self-efficacy was a prevalent theme. For example, Gail noted, "Fear of saying the wrong thing. It is a big responsibility." Similarly, Candice wrote, "I'm not famous or interesting enough." Phoebe stated a barrier she faced was "comfortability in front of the camera."

RQ4: effective and ineffective communication techniques

Residents identified three key skills germane to advocacy communication, following the workshop: cocreation, clarity, and audience-centeredness. In describing the cocreation of meaning, participants used words such as connecting, understanding, and closing the loop in communication. For example, Edward said, "speaking on the same level with empathy" and Phoebe described it as, "like two people walking away from a discussion understanding the other's goals/point and feeling as if the discussion was useful." Dawn described this as, "Meeting patients at their level. Phrases and analogies that they understand, and constantly pausing to assess their understanding." Beth said that effective communication was "having the audience understand the message and be able to teach back … " On the negative side, Vicki described ineffective communication as "steamrolling an interaction."

Clarity was another common theme participants identified as effective communication (and the lack of clarity was identified as ineffective). Rachel, for example, described ineffective communication as "overly detailed or complicated," Candice described a lack of clarity as, "the information is perceived in an unintended way or not received at all." Conversely, Rachel called effective communication, "clear, concise, and easy to relate to." Trisha described effective communication as simply "clear and concise," and ineffective communication as "not clarifying question or points, making assumptions, laziness." Frances described his approach: "I try to simplify my message and tailor my phrasing based upon the level of sophistication of the audience."

Participants also identified audience-centeredness as a key aspect of effective communication. For example, Jennifer said, "paying attention to your audience, back and forth, both contributing and listening," and Vicki explained effective communication as "give and take, reading the audience." Dawn said it was "using phrases and analogies that [the audience] can understand." The notion of audience-centeredness was embedded in all of Phoebe's responses. She described effective communication as "walking away from a discussion understanding the other's goals/point and feeling as if the discussion was useful," and ineffective communication as, "when one party feels an inability to communicate effectively or feels as if the discussion was not valuable." (Table 3).

Discussion

This research sought to fill a gap in the literature by closely examining a pedagogical intervention (AIT) designed to teach advocacy communication to pediatric residents. Because

Table 3. Research questions, qualitative themes, and representative examples.

Research question	Theme	Example from participant quotations
RQ1: Willingness and Ability to Advocate in Media and Community	Organization-Based Advocacy	Role on a hospital-based patient safety advocacy committee
	Individual Advocacy	I had the ability to contact my state senator regarding topics that I have felt strongly about
RQ2: Sustained Communication Techniques	Message Distillation	I try to simplify my message and tailor my phrasing based upon the level of sophistication of the audience
	Empathy	I think I try to understand ore where the other person is coming from and what their goals are
	Language Transformation	I try to tailor my phrasing based upon the level of sophistication of the audience
RQ3: Ongoing Barriers to Communicating with the Media	Time and Opportunity	
	Self-Efficacy	Fear of saying the wrong thing. It is a big responsibility
RQ4: Effective and Ineffective Communication Techniques	Co-Creation	Like two people walking away from a discussion understanding the other's goals/point and feeling as if the discussion was useful
	Clarity	Using phrases and analogies that they can understand
	Audience-Centeredness	Paying attention to your audience, back and forth, both contributing and listening

AIT has been used in a number of other settings, we found it important to investigate to what extent an instructional intervention like this could be helpful in the health care setting, given the changing relationship between the media and the public and therefore the need for ongoing communication flexibility of health care professionals. Future physicians, especially pediatricians, face growing communication challenges. They increasingly need to move outside the patient room to effectively connect with an ever-more skeptical public. Applied improvisation training offers unique complements to more traditional CST and is particularly powerful in addressing these challenges by emphasizing dynamic responsiveness, empathetic connection, and audience-centeredness. As our training program illustrated, these skills helped pediatric residents reframe conversations to ensure both parties work toward the same goals, providing them with an agility not afforded by traditional CST.

Our survey data consistently demonstrated that our residents found the workshop to be worthwhile and effective. Moreover, at long term follow-up, they identified cocreation of meaning as a key component of effective communication, which was central to the larger, overarching instructional goal of the AIT workshop. Finally, results suggest that residents did incorporate topics from the training into their day-to-day interactions. These results further evidence what others have found: communication instruction can successfully alter participants behavior (Brown et al., 2010; Cegala & Lenzmeier Broz, 2002). After completing our program, resident physicians consistently felt they were better prepared to engage in advocacy work, including interacting with the media.

Even though this workshop was effective in providing learners with new tools to communicate more confidently, it is important to note that it did not, on its own, provide residents with the degree of self-efficacy some believed they needed to fully see themselves as an advocate. We see this as an important theoretical implication warranting further exploration. Our participants were interested in participating in advocacy; however, they lacked the self-efficacy needed to fully embrace that role. Although we would argue this is a lofty goal to accomplish in a single-day workshop, there are interesting theoretical considerations worth exploring considering this finding. Questions for further exploration, drawing on CMM (Pearce, 2007; Pearce & Cronen, 1980), include: What communicative patterns and context have created this lack of self-efficacy in resident physicians? What is the role of self-efficacy in advocacy communication? How could we design resident and physician training programs to improve self-efficacy, given the multiple, complex stories that characterize provider–patient–public relationships?

Furthermore, the advocacy approach championed by Hubinette et al. (2017) may be missing this key aspect of advocacy communication (self-efficacy). Perhaps many novice physicians do not feel comfortable directing advocacy efforts because of their perceived lack of experience and expertise. For residents to feel comfortable in a public advocacy forum, they must view themselves as experts, and this is not something a person can develop quickly. Instructional programs using AIT may be one step in this direction, but further research should explore these issues in more depth.

Limitations and future research

Our program differed from many other training programs for physicians in that we focused on advocacy communication for pediatric residents, as opposed to patient–provider communication and the physician population in general. Additionally, we used AIT as a tool to improve residents' communication skills, rather than traditional CST. These two approaches, though relatively successful in this context, also invite some limitations and opportunities for future research. As mentioned, there is still a fair amount of definitional work required to understand advocacy communication by health professionals and our study did not fully explore these definitional distinctions. For example, in what ways is advocacy communication similar to and different from patient–provider communication and how might training be modified based on these differences? Given that advocacy rotations are required of pediatric residents, it is important that we continue to pursue these definitions while still providing training to these junior physicians. Similarly, resident physicians are very new to the practice of medicine. So, it is no surprise that their confidence is limited. Future research could explore how more veteran practitioners might respond to training such as this. That said, AIT as a teaching tool can be difficult for some audiences to accept (Berk & Trieber, 2009; Hoffmann-Longtin et al., 2018). Additional investigation is needed to understand the circumstances under which training audiences would be comfortable accepting this approach. The length of our training program (one day) also creates a limitation. It is challenging to argue such a short intervention would create significant differences in behavior. More locations, types, and lengths of instructional programs would help us to answer some of the questions posed by Donovan et al. (2017) about which types of communication training are most efficacious in health contexts. Finally, we used self-report data from our residents to evaluate the AIT training program, thus inviting a social desirability bias of our participants simply saying what we want to hear. While these data are generally appropriate for program evaluation, their utility in the broader context of communication training efficacy is limited. Future research could include independent researcher observations or patients' reporting of the residents' skills both before and after the intervention.

Implications for teaching and learning in health contexts

Although our study does have limitations, we believe it offers a new and innovative approach to teaching advocacy communication to pediatric residents. More broadly, our study offers three important implications for communication scholars who teach and research in healthcare settings. First, we would encourage scholars to use extant communication theory to problematize overly simplistic definitions of communication in medicine. As Egener and Cole-Kelly (2004) argued, it is certainly possible to pass the test but fail the patient when communicating in healthcare contexts. Health information and the healthcare system are too complex to understand using simplistic definitions, and several communication theories could be fruitful in helping change the perceptions of those who believe communication is simplistic. With that in mind, our study illustrates that resident physicians are willing to accept and apply more complex, social constructionist definitions of communication. By designing programs with these kinds of theoretical approaches, we can give physicians language and tools to address what many already know all too well: communicating effectively is one of the hardest parts of their jobs.

Secondly, communication scholars have an opportunity to help healthcare practitioners realize that their communication skills beyond the bedside are worth focus and attention. So much research has been conducted on the effectiveness of health messages, yet many nonacademic physicians know little about this work. Given the calls for pediatricians to serve as advocates for children's health, they must be effective advocacy communicators as well. By providing training that focuses specifically on advocacy settings—and on audience analysis and message distillation within those settings—we can help physicians see that public communication is a key part of the job that is as high stakes as bedside communication.

Lastly, we hope this study encourages communication scholars to consider creative approaches to teaching communication, particularly in healthcare settings. Many traditional approaches to CST need to be reconsidered, given the need to help physicians enact the empathy and dynamic responsiveness necessary to address today's complicated healthcare environment and media landscape. By employing AIT, we hope to illustrate how these creative approaches can help deconstruct some of the structures that prevent skill development. We hope future scholars and teachers will bring in additional creative pedagogical approaches to the health care setting.

Conclusions

The AIT instructional intervention, which is at the center of this study, focused on encouraging pediatric residents to redefine advocacy communication as cocreation of meaning, rather than simple information transfer. Through a day-long AIT workshop, we sought to increase pediatric residents' responsiveness, empathetic connection, and audience-centeredness. This kind of skill development is critical, given today's healthcare communication landscape. Patients often come to their physician with information (sometimes incorrect) obtained from social media and Internet searches, as well as friends, family, and community groups. Physicians have the daunting task of helping patients to interpret this information, while building trust and confidence. This responsibility extends beyond the patient room. Physicians are asked to serve as health experts in community settings and the news media. They are called upon by their professional organizations to advocate for improved health policies and systems of care. In short, physicians are asked to do more than simply deliver information. They must serve as advocates for accurate information and healthy habits, at the bedside and in the community.

As our data and the work of others in the field indicate, CST programs can improve physician communication skills. By understanding the basis on which health decisions are made and offering opportunities for context-based practice, instructional programs using AIT can provide residents with a platform to explore their own perceptions of communication and develop the dynamic communication skills needed to advocate effectively in a variety of contexts. In doing so, perhaps training programs such as this one—that employ creative pedagogical approaches—can assist physicians in better navigating complexities of the healthcare communication environment that can paralyze novice and experienced physicians alike. As Spolin (1999), widely considered the foremother of improvisational theater, suggested, "When it bogs down, play a game" (xiii). An experiential, game-based approach to communication training, like AIT, may have the potential to help physicians improve the bogged down healthcare environment, by working in partnership with their patients for better health outcomes.

Notes

1. The survey was developed for program assessment purposes and would need further refinement and validation if it were to be used in the future for additional research purposes.
2. The full surveys are available from the first author upon request.

Acknowledgements

The authors would like to thank the two anonymous reviewers and editors for their comments, which greatly improved the manuscript.

Funding

This work was supported by Indiana University School of Medicine Department of Pediatrics.

ORCID

Krista Hoffmann-Longtin http://orcid.org/0000-0002-5625-3977
Jason M. Organ http://orcid.org/0000-0001-8462-0271
Elizabeth Weinstein http://orcid.org/0000-0002-6074-0604

References

Accreditation Council on Graduate Medical Education (ACGME). (2017). *Program requirements for graduate medical education in pediatrics.* Retrieved from: http://www.acgme.org/Portals/0/PFAssets/ProgramRequirements/320_pediatrics_2017-07-01.pdf?ver=2017-06-30-083432-507

American Academy of Pediatrics (AAP). (2018). *Advocacy and policy.* Retrieved from: https://www.aap.org

Association of American Medical Colleges (AAMC). (2015). Active physicians by sex and specialty, 2015. *AAMC Data and Reports.* Retrieved from: https://www.aamc.org/data/workforce/reports/458712/1-3chart.html

Berk, R. A., & Trieber, R. H. (2009). Whose classroom is it, anyway? Improvisation as a teaching tool. *Journal on Excellence in College Teaching, 20*(3), 29–60.

Boesen, K. P., Herrier, R. N., Apgar, D. A., & Jackowski, R. M. (2009). Improvisational exercises to improve pharmacy students' professional communication skills. *American Journal of Pharmacy Education, 27*, 1–8.

Brown, P., Zavestoski, S., McCormick, S., Mayer, B., Morello-Frosch, R., & Gasior Altman, R. (2004). Embodied health movements: New approaches to social movements in health. *Sociology of Health & Illness, 26*(1), 50–80.

Brown, R. F., & Bylund, C. L. (2008). Communication skills training: Describing a new conceptual model. *Academic Medicine, 83*, 37–44.

Brown, R. F., Bylund, C. L., Gueguen, J. A., Diamond, C., Eddington, J., & Kissane, D. (2010). Developing patient-centered communication skills training for oncologists: Describing the content and efficacy of training. *Communication Education, 59*(3), 235–248. doi:10.1080/03634521003606210

Cegala, D. J., & Lenzmeier Broz, S. (2002). Physician communication skills training: A review of the theoretical backgrounds, objectives and skills. *Medical Education, 36*, 1004–1016.

Deveugele, M., Derese, A., De Maesschalck, S., Willems, S., Van Driel, M., & De Maeseneer, J. (2005). Teaching communication skills to medical students, a challenge in the curriculum? *Patient Education and Counseling, 58*(3), 265–270.

Donovan, E., Love, B., Mackert, M., Vangelisti, A., & Ring, D. (2017). Health communication: A future direction for instructional communication research. *Communication Education, 66*(4), 490–492.

Dworkis, D. A., Wilbur, M. B., & Sandel, M. T. (2010). A framework for designing training in medical advocacy. *Academic Medicine, 85*(10), 1549–1550.

Earnest, M. A., Wong, S. L., & Federico, S. G. (2010). Physician advocacy: What is it and how do we do it? *Academic Medicine, 85*(1), 63–67.

Egener, B., & Cole-Kelly, K. (2004). Satisfying the patient, but failing the test. *Academic Medicine, 79*(6), 508–510.

Eisenberg, A., Rosenthal, S., & Schlussel, Y. R. (2015). Medicine as a performing art: What we can learn about empathic communication from theater arts. *Academic Medicine, 90*(3), 272–276.

Frenk, J., Chen, L., Bhutta, Z. A., Cohen, J., Crisp, N., Evans, T., … Zurayk, H. (2010). Health professionals for a new century: Transforming education to strengthen health systems in an interdependent world. *Lancet, 376*(9756), 1923–1958.

Funk, C. (2017, February 9). Parents of young children are more 'vaccine hesitant'. *Pew Research Center Fact Tank*. Retrieved from: http://www.pewresearch.org

Gruen, R. L., Campbell, E. G., & Blumenthal, D. (2006). Public roles of US physicians: Community participation, political involvement, and collective advocacy. *Journal of the American Medical Association, 296*, 2467–2475.

Gysels, M., Richardson, A., & Higginson, I. J. (2004). Communication training for health professionals who care for patients with cancer: A systematic review of effectiveness. *Supportive Care in Cancer, 12*, 692–700.

Hanley, M., & Fenton, M. V. (2007). Exploring improvisation in nursing. *Journal of Holistic Nursing, 25*, 126–133.

Hoffmann-Longtin, K., Rossing, J. P., & Donovan, E. (2018). *Communication theory, applied improvisation, and communication competence across the disciplines.* Manuscript presented at the National Communication Association meeting in Salt Lake City, UT.

Hoffmann-Longtin, K., Rossing, J. P., & Weinstein, E. (2018). Twelve tips for using applied improvisation in medical education. *Medical Teacher, 40*(4), 351–356. doi:10.1080/0142159X.2017.1387239

Hubinette, M., Dobson, S., Scott, I., & Sherbino, J. (2017). Health advocacy. *Medical Teacher, 39*(2), 128–135.

Jagodowski, T. J., & Pasquesi, D. (2015). *Improvisation at the speed of life*. Chicago, IL: Solo Roma.

Kanter, S. L. (2011). On physician advocacy. *Academic Medicine, 86*(9), 1059–1060.

Kaplan-Liss, E., Lantz-Gefroh, V., Bass, E., Killebrew, D., Ponzio, N. M., Savi, C., & O'Connell, C. (2018). Teaching medical students to communicate with empathy and clarity using improvisation. *Academic Medicine, 93*(3), 440–443. doi:10.1097/ACM.0000000000002031

Konnikova, M. (2014, July 16). Being a better online reader. *The New Yorker*. Retrieved from: https://www.newyorker.com/science/maria-konnikova/being-a-better-online-reader

Kurtz, S., Draper, J., & Silverman, J. (Eds.). (2004). *Teaching and learning communication skills in medicine* (2nd ed.). London: CRC Press.

Lee, C., & Hornik, R. C. (2009). Physician trust moderates the internet use and physician visit relationship. *Journal of Health Communication, 14*(1), 70–76. doi:10.1080/10810730802592262

Levinson, W., Lesser, C. S., & Epstein, R. M. (2010). Developing physician communication skills for patient-centered care. *Health Affairs, 29*(7), 1310–1318.

Lichtenstein, C., Hoffman, B. D., & Moon, R. Y. (2017). How do US pediatric residency programs teach and evaluate community pediatrics and advocacy training? *Academic Pediatrics, 17*(5), 544–549. doi:10.1016/j.acap.2017.02.011

Lincoln, Y. S., & Guba, E. G. (1985). *Naturalistic inquiry*. Newbury Park, CA: Sage.

Makoul, G. (2001). Essential elements of communication in medical encounters: The Kalamazoo consensus statement. *Academic Medicine, 76*(4), 390–393.

Makoul, G., & Schofield, T. (1999). Communication teaching and assessment in medical education: An international consensus statement. *Patient Education and Counseling, 137*, 191–195.

Martin, D., & Whitehead, C. (2013). Physician, healthy system: The challenge of training doctor-citizens. *Medical Teacher, 35*, 416–417.

Patton, M. Q. (2002). *Qualitative research and evaluation methods* (3rd ed.). Thousand Oaks, CA: Sage.

Pearce, W. B. (1989). *Communication and the human condition*. Carbondale, IL: Southern Illinois University Press.

Pearce, W. B. (2004). *Using CMM: The coordinated management of meaning*. San Mateo, CA: Pearce Associates. Retrieved from: http://www.pearceassociates.com/essays/cmm_seminar.pdf

Pearce, W. B. (2007). *Making social worlds: A communication perspective*. Malden, MA: Blackwell Publishing.

Pearce, W. B., & Cronen, V. (1980). *Communication, action, and meaning: The creation of social realities*. New York, NY: Praeger.

Rider, E. A., & Keefer, C. H. (2006). Communication skills competencies: Definitions and a teaching toolbox. *Medical Education, 40*(7), 624–629.

Rosenbaum, L. (2017). Resisting the suppression of science. *New England Journal of Medicine, 376*, 1607–1609. doi:10.1056/NEJMp1702362

Rossing, J. P., & Hoffmann-Longtin, K. (2016). Improv(ing) the academy: Applied improvisation as a tool in educational development. *To Improve the Academy, 35*(20), 303–325. doi:10.1002/tia2.20044

Salmon, P., & Young, B. (2011). Creativity in clinical communication: From communication skills to skilled communication. *Medical Education, 45*, 217–226. doi:10.1111/j.1365-2923.2010.03801.x

Satcher, D., Kaczorowski, J., & Topa, D. (2005). The expanding role of the pediatrician in improving child health in the 21st century. *Pediatrics, 115*(Supplement 3), 1124–1128.

Sawyer, K. R. (2011). *Structure and improvisation in creative teaching*. Cambridge: Cambridge University Press.

Sawyer, T., Fu, B., Gray, M., & Umoren, R. (2017). Medical improvisation training to enhance the antenatal counseling skills of neonatologists and neonatal fellows: A pilot study. *The Journal of Maternal-Fetal & Neonatal Medicine, 30*(15), 1865–1869. doi:10.1080/14767058.2016.1228059

Scinto, J. (2014). Why improv training is great business training. *Forbes*. Retrieved from: http://www.forbes.com/sites/forbesleadershipforum/2014/06/27/why-improv-training-is-great-business-training/

Shipley, L. J., Stelzner, S. M., Zenni, E. A., Hargunani, D., O'Keefe, J., Miller, C., ... Swigonski, N. (2005). Teaching community pediatrics to pediatric residents: Strategic approaches and successful models for education in community health and child advocacy. *Pediatrics, 115*, 1150–1157.

Spolin, V. (1999). *Improvisation for the theater: A handbook of teaching and directing techniques*. Evanston, IL: Northwestern University Press.

Watson, K. (2011). Serious play: Teaching medical skills with improvisational theater techniques. *Academic Medicine, 86*(10), 1260–1265.

Watzlawick, P., Beavin, J. H., & Jackson, D. D. (1967). *Pragmatics of human communication.* New York, NY: Norton.

Zoller, H. M. (2005). Health activism: Communication theory and action for social change. *Communication Theory, 15*(4), 341–364.

Zoppi, K., & Epstein, R. M. (2002). Is communication a skill? Communication behaviours and being in relation. *Family Medicine, 34*, 319–324.

Fake news, phishing, and fraud: a call for research on digital media literacy education beyond the classroom

Nicole M. Lee

ABSTRACT
The Internet poses a variety of risks at both the individual and societal levels including scams and the spread of misinformation. Older adults are especially vulnerable to many of these risks. This paper argues that one important strategy for combating such threats is through digital media literacy education. Although a good deal of research on digital media literacy for children exists, very little research exists on effective digital media literacy instructional interventions for adult populations. Specific directions for future research are offered.

Recent events, such as the spread of false online news during the 2016 U.S. presidential election and Cambridge Analytica's use of private Facebook data to influence American voters, have highlighted some of the risks related to relying on and engaging with online information. Along with the issues of misinformation and privacy, cybercrimes such as phishing and other types of fraud continue to increase (Federal Bureau of Investigation [FBI], 2017). Advancing digital media literacy can help people understand these threats and better evaluate information and sources.

Media literacy is an individual's ability to access, analyze, and evaluate media (Aufderheide, 1993). Media literacy instruction may ask audiences to consider factors such as who is sending a message, the purpose of a message, the persuasive techniques included, and the potential interpretations of a message—skills crucial in the current digital media environment (Hobbs, 2007). Although digital media literacy has become a major focus of media literacy research in recent decades (Kamerer, 2013), this scholarship focuses primarily on social media safety for children and adolescents (e.g., Agosto & Abbas, 2016).

However, fake news, scams, phishing, and other risks faced by those interacting with information and sources on digital platforms often target not children but adults. nondigital natives, and older adults in particular, are a vulnerable population when it comes to online risks (vulnerable populations are defined as those most susceptible to harm in any given context; Mechanic & Tanner, 2007). In 2016, there were more cybercrimes (55,043) committed against people 60 years and older than any other age group (FBI, 2017). Crimes against people in their 30s (54,670), 40s (51,394), and 50s (49,208) were not far behind. Although reported crimes span age groups, according to the FBI, older Americans are less likely to report scams because they are ashamed or do not want family members to think their mental capacities are declining (FBI, n.d.). Because adults, and specifically older adults, are in need of digital media literacy programs, and because many of these adults are not engaged in traditional academic classrooms, this paper is a call for more research on effective digital media literacy interventions outside the traditional classroom.

Need for digital media literacy instruction outside the traditional classroom

Not all cybercrimes are avoidable, but many that rely on individuals trusting fraudulent websites, emails, or social media accounts could be countered through education. For example, phishing typically occurs when a fraudulent entity disguised as a legitimate organization emails a victim and asks for personal information or their password (FBI, 2017). Such a crime depends on potential victims not knowing how to verify the source of an email. Similarly, fraudulent social media accounts may promote sweepstakes or even fundraisers to collect personal information or money from unsuspecting social media users. One prominent example of such a scam was a series of posts circulated on Facebook that claimed Southwest Airlines was giving away free airline tickets to anyone who took a short survey, liked the post, shared it, and left a comment. One Facebook post that was created and shared as part of this scam received more than 80,000 comments (Wade, 2017).

Although many digital media cybercrimes target individuals, misinformation disseminated through social media channels can have consequences for national politics and international relations, as well. During the 2016 U.S. presidential election, fake news, or false information presented as news, became a prominent topic in public discourse, in part because of its potential impact on the outcome of the election (Allcott & Gentzkow, 2017). Some political figures have referred to legitimate news sources as fake news in an attempt to discredit unflattering media coverage (Vernon, 2017), but for the purposes of this paper, I use the term fake news to refer to actual misinformation.

False news stories are not entirely new, but the scale of the issue in 2016 brought it to the forefront of political discussion (Allcott & Gentzkow, 2017). A majority of social media users report encountering fake news, and many also admit to believing the false information they see (Silverman & Singer-Vine, 2016). During the 2016 election, the most widely shared fake news posts on Facebook were reposted more than the most popular news stories from legitimate outlets (Silverman, 2016). For example, one of the most shared fake news stories was an article claiming that the Pope had endorsed Donald Trump for president. The motives behind the propaganda have also been a cause for concern. According to U.S. intelligence agencies, Russia created and distributed fake news stories on social media in order to influence the U.S. presidential election and disrupt the democratic process (Intelligence Community Assessment [ICA], 2017).

A call for research: nondigital natives and digital media literacy

Despite these issues, there is a paucity of research on effective strategies for educating adults in general and nondigital natives in particular about safe social media use, including protecting one's privacy, recognizing false information, and avoiding scams. According to

Hobbs (2005), media literacy education should help individuals analyze social, economic, political, and historical factors that influence media. For example, understanding that the way headlines are written can be influenced by the need for link clicks to drive ad revenue. Bringing these factors to the forefront could help Internet users become critical consumers of online media information and sources. Although this topic is undoubtedly interdisciplinary, communication and instructional scholars have a unique opportunity to make an important contribution to research in this area as it pertains to teaching and learning processes both within and beyond traditional classrooms. As with any communication research, it is important to know which channels, sources, and message types are most influential. In addition to the practical implications, examining these phenomena and studying adult populations will advance media literacy research and inform theory. Specifically, I encourage research in three areas related to digital media literacy: evaluating information and sources, protecting privacy and safe social media use, and avoiding scams and phishing.

Evaluating information and sources

The moniker is often debated, but most agree that fake news or misinformation distributed online is an issue that must be addressed. Fake news can fall into several categories including satire, hoaxes, and propaganda (Dicker, 2016). Although the purpose of satire is not to mislead the audience, social media users often mistake satirical articles for actual news. Hoaxes are fake news stories that are meant to mislead people, often to generate web traffic, but do not have a political motivation. Propaganda is arguably the biggest threat because it is the use of misinformation or misleading information for political purposes, such as the use of fabricated online stories by Russian agents during the 2016 election (ICA, 2017). Misinformation can potentially sway elections (Gunther, Beck, & Nisbet, 2018), increase political polarization (Flaxman, Goel, & Rao, 2016), and even lead to violence (Haag & Salam, 2017).

Research on the effects of false information suggests that media literacy education may be an effective means of mitigating the harm. Prior studies have found that it can be very difficult to undo the effects of misinformation once individuals believe it to be true (Lewandowsky, Ecker, Seifert, Schwarz, & Cook, 2012) and that fact-checking can even have backfire effects (Nyhan & Reifler, 2010). Rather than correcting false information, teaching audiences to be skeptical may be a more effective approach for combating fake news. The news media have provided some guidelines and warnings for avoiding fake news (e.g., Thurrott, 2018), but these have mostly been one-off reports that Internet users must take the initiative to seek out themselves. Although there are resources available, further research should inform which messages are most effective and how best to deliver them to the general adult population.

A first step for this research could be to test and evaluate existing materials such as a video created by FactCheck.org (FlackCheck, 2016) or resources created by the Center for News Literacy at Stony Brook University (Center for News Literacy, n.d.). Doing so may help researchers determine whether effective instructional materials already exist and inform further examination of the best distribution methods. A meta-analysis of media literacy research found that media literacy interventions are typically more effective across multiple sessions (Jeong, Cho, & Hwang, 2012). However, that can be particularly challenging outside a traditional classroom setting. Research should test whether that finding applies to media literacy interventions outside the classroom and, if so, how best to encourage participants to engage with educational materials over time. For instance, researchers could compare a one-day workshop at a community center with a series of shorter workshops that cover the same material but over the course of several weeks. Researchers could compare how effective each format is in producing the desired affective, cognitive, and behavioral learning outcomes; the retention of these learning outcomes over time; and attrition rate for the longer series.

Additionally, years of media effects research has demonstrated the importance of individual differences when it comes to the effectiveness of media messages (Oliver, 2002). Future research should examine the demographics and psychographics that may influence the effectiveness of these interventions with adult populations. Specifically, studies can explore variables such as political ideology, innate skepticism, age, and gender. For example, are older adults more likely to prefer print materials? Or, will certain sources of information (e.g., academics or government agencies) be less effective depending on participants' political ideology?

Protecting privacy and safe social media use

Social media, and the self-disclosure that often comes with it, can lead to an array of privacy and safety concerns, including social, financial, and physical risks. Because of the nature of social networking sites, users feel compelled to share information about themselves to build social capital (Ellison, Vitak, Steinfield, Gray, & Lampe, 2011). However, disclosing information such as birthdates, phone numbers, maiden names, and addresses can open users to identity fraud (Acquisti & Gross, 2006). According to Javelin Strategy & Research (Pascual, Marchini, & Miller, 2018), 16.7 million people fell victim to identity fraud in 2017. Moreover, children and older adults were among the most frequently targeted. Users also commonly share information about vacations and travel plans in real time, which can leave them and their homes at risk for crime. According to law enforcement (Holmes, 2018) and a survey of convicted burglars (Glorioso, Wallace, & Manney, 2016), thieves often use social media posts to determine whom to target.

Previous research reveals that there is little relationship between privacy concerns and social media users' disclosure behaviors (Tufekci, 2008). This suggests that simply making people aware of the risk is not adequate for changing behavior. Future research should test which types of interventions may be more effective at producing the desired affective, cognitive, and behavioral learning outcomes. Literature on risk communication is one area that could inform research in this area. Risk communication researchers have examined a variety of areas including health and safety topics ranging from food safety (e.g., Sellnow, Lane, Sellnow, & Littlefield, 2017) to terrorism (e.g., Palenchar, Heath, & Orberton, 2005).

One approach could be to test Protection Motivation Theory (PMT) in the context of Internet risks. PMT (Rogers, 1983) suggests that audiences react to fear appeals by evaluating both the threat and their ability to respond to the threat. Through examining perceptions of threat severity (seriousness), threat susceptibility (likelihood), response efficacy (effectiveness of response behaviors), and self-efficacy (ability to perform the response behavior), scholars could help inform educational communication campaigns or other interventions targeting adult populations outside traditional classrooms. For example, research may find that users recognize the severity of the threat and their susceptibility to it, but also do not think they can do anything about it. Conversely, research could find that participants do not believe they are susceptible to the threat and therefore see no reason to act. Understanding where the knowledge gaps are may help scholars design effective instructional materials.

Avoiding scams and phishing

Hundreds of thousands of U.S. adults fall victim to online scams each year. These scams affect adults of all ages but crimes against those 60 years and older are the most common (FBI, 2017). Phishing and other types of cyber scams accounted for $1.33 billion in victim losses in 2016. In fact, those 60 years and older alone lost $339 million; these are victims who are often on fixed incomes. The FBI also estimates that only 15 percent of victims report their crimes and that older adults are particularly unlikely to do so.

Research should strive to better understand how to protect this vulnerable population against these risks. Scholarship on education for older adults can lend some guidance but studies in this area are limited and often focus on health education. Research on learning motivations among older adults has found that keeping an active mind and being a lifelong learner are key drivers of the desire to partake in educational activities (Boulton-Lewis, Buys, & Lovie-Kitchin, 2006). Tapping into such motivations could inform instructional communication strategies for gaining interest in online safety programing. For instance, researchers could compare turn out and attrition for two workshops—one framed as an opportunity to learn for the intrinsic value and the other framed as an extrinsic need to protect oneself online.

Considerations for digital media literacy beyond the traditional classroom

Several different sampling and data collection methods, including online surveys using Amazon Mechanical Turk or third-party research firms, could be useful for conducting research on adult populations. However, those methods may not be appropriate for older adults or those less comfortable with technology. Alternatively, researchers could test different types of curricula in different community centers or senior living facilities. Research with aging populations carries unique challenges in terms of recruitment. Scholars pursuing such research should be mindful of recommendations from past research such as building long-term relationships within the community and offering appropriate incentives to participants to show that their time is valued (Weil, Mendoza, & McGavin, 2017).

Conclusion

We are living in an age when some of the greatest threats we face daily are unseen and poorly understood. Internet users of all ages make mistakes when it comes to what messages and sources to trust, as well as what information is safe to disclose and where. These kinds of risks present an opportunity—and a responsibility—for communication researchers to engage in high impact research for the good of society. Although many are already doing just that, there is room to do more; in particular, we can make a significant contribution to the scholarly conversation if we extend the focus of digital media literacy scholarship and pedagogy to older adult populations for whom this work can lead to an improved quality of life.

ORCID

Nicole M. Lee ⓘ http://orcid.org/0000-0003-3101-4969

References

Acquisti, A., & Gross, R. (2006). Imagined communities: Awareness, information sharing, and privacy on the facebook. In *Privacy enhancing technologies: 6th international workshop, PET 2006,* (pp. 26–58). Cambridge: Springer.

Agosto, D. E., & Abbas, J. (2016). Simple tips for helping students become safer, smarter social media users. *Knowledge Quest, 44*(42), 42–47.

Allcott, H., & Gentzkow, M. (2017). Social media and fake news in the 2016 election. *Journal of Economic Perspectives, 31,* 211–236. doi:10.1257/jep.31.2.211

Aufderheide, P. (1993). *Media literacy: A report of the national leadership conference on media literacy.* Aspen, CO: Aspen Institute.

Boulton-Lewis, G. M., Buys, L., & Lovie-Kitchin, J. (2006). Learning and active aging. *Educational Gerontology, 32,* 271–282. doi:10.1080/03601270500494030

Center for News Literacy. (n.d.). *Getting started.* Retrieved from http://www.centerfornewsliteracy.org

Dicker, R. (2016, November 14). Avoid these fake news sites at all costs. *U.S. News and World Report.* Retrieved from https://www.usnews.com

Ellison, N. B., Vitak, J., Steinfield, C., Gray, R., & Lampe, C. (2011). Negotiating privacy concerns and social capital needs in a social media environment. In S. Trepte, & L. Reinecke (Eds.), *Privacy online.* (pp. 19–32). Berlin, Germany: Springer.

Federal Bureau of Investigation. (n.d.). *Fraud against seniors.* Retrieved from https://www.fbi.gov

Federal Bureau of Investigation/Internet Crime Complaint Center. (2017). *2016 internet crime report.* Washington, DC: FBI.

FlackCheck. (2016, December 8). *How to spot fake news – Factcheck.org* [Video File]. Retrieved from https://www.youtube.com/watch?v=AkwWcHekMdo

Flaxman, S., Goel, S., & Rao, J. M. (2016). Filter bubbles, echo chambers, and online news consumption. *Public Opinion Quarterly, 80,* 298–320. doi:10.1093/poq/nfw006

Glorioso, C., Wallace, S., & Manney, D. (2016, August 22). I-Team: Convicted burglars reveal how they case their targets. *NBC 4 New York.* Retrieved from https://www.nbcnewyork.com

Gunther, R., Beck, P. A., & Nisbet, E. C. (2018). *Fake news did have a significant impact on the vote in the 2016 election: Original full-length version with methodological appendix.* Retrieved from https://u.osu.edu/cnep/files/2015/03/Fake-News-Piecefor-The-Conversation-with-methodological-appendix-11d0ni9.pdf

Haag, M., & Salam, M. (2017, June 22). Gunman in 'Pizzagate' shooting is sentenced to 4 years in prison. *New York Times.* Retrieved from https://www.nytimes.com

Hobbs, R. (2005). The state of media literacy education. *Journal of Communication, 55,* 865–871.

Hobbs, R. (2007). *Reading the media: Media literacy in high school English.* New York: Teachers College Press.

Holmes, B. (2018, April 19). Police warn about mix of social media and vacations. *North Reading Patch.* Retrieved from https://patch.com/massachusetts/northreading/police-warn-mix-social-media-vacations

Intelligence Community Assessment. (2017). Background to "Assessing Russian activities and intentions in recent US elections": The analytic process and cyber incident attribution. Retrieved from https://www.dni.gov/files/documents/ICA_2017_01.pdf

Jeong, S., Cho, H., & Hwang, Y. (2012). Media literacy interventions: A meta-analytic review. *Journal of Communication, 62,* 454–472. doi:10.1111/j.1460-2466.2012.01643.x

Kamerer, D. (2013). Media literacy. *Communication Research Trends, 32,* 4–25.

Lewandowsky, S., Ecker, U. K. H., Seifert, C. M., Schwarz, N., & Cook, J. (2012). Misinformation and its correction: Continued influence and successful debiasing. *Psychological Science in the Public Interest, 13,* 106–131. doi:10.1177/1529100612451018

Mechanic, D., & Tanner, J. (2007). Vulnerable people, groups, and populations: Societal view. *Health Affairs, 26,* 1220–1230. doi:10.1377/hlthaff.26.5.1220

Nyhan, B., & Reifler, J. (2010). When corrections fail: The persistence of political misperceptions. *Political Behavior, 32,* 303–330. doi:10.1007/s11109-010-9112-2

Oliver, M. B. (2002). Individual differences in media effects. In J. Bryant, & D. Zillmann (Eds.), *Media effects: Advances in theory and research* (pp. 507–524). Mahwah, NJ: Lawrence Erlbaum Associates Publishers.

Palenchar, M., Heath, R., & Orberton, E. (2005). Terrorism and industrial chemical production: A new era of risk communication. *Communication Research Reports, 22,* 59–67. doi:10.1080/00036810500059886

Pascual, A., Marchini, K., & Miller, S. (2018). *2018 identity fraud: Fraud enters a new era of complexity.* Pleasanton, CA: Javelin Strategy & Research.

Rogers, R. W. (1983). Cognitive and physiological processes in fear appeals and attitude change: A revised theory of protection motivation. In J. Cacioppo, & R. Petty (Eds.), *Social psychophysiology,* 153–176. New York: Guilford Press.

Sellnow, D. D., Lane, D. R., Sellnow, T. L., & Littlefield, R. S. (2017). The IDEA model as a best practice for effective instructional risk and crisis communication. *Communication Studies, 68,* 552–567. doi:0.1080/10510974.2017.1375535

Silverman, C. (2016, November 16). This analysis shows how viral fake election news stories outperformed real news on Facebook. *Buzzfeed.* Retrieved from https://www.buzzfeed.com

Silverman, C., & Singer-Vine, J. (2016, December 6). Most Americans who see fake news believe it, new survey says. *Buzzfeed.* Retrieved from https://www.buzzfeed.com

Thurrott, S. (2018, March 13). How to spot fake news in your social media feed. *NBC News.* Retrieved from https://www.nbcnews.com

Tufekci, Z. (2008). Can you see me now? Audience and disclosure regulation in online social network sites. *Bulletin of Science, Technology & Society, 11,* 544–564. doi:10.1177/0270467607311484

Vernon, P. (2017, January 11). Trump berated a CNN reporter, and fellow journalists missed an opportunity. *Columbia Journalism Review.* Retrieved from https://www.cjr.org

Wade, C. (2017, December 11). Don't fall for a fake Southwest Air 'free ticket' Facebook scam. *CBS DFW.* Retrieved from http://dfw.cbslocal.com

Weil, J., Mendoza, A. N., & McGavin, E. (2017). Recruiting older adults as participants in applied social research: Applying and evaluating approaches from clinical studies. *Educational Gerontology, 43,* 662–673. doi:10.1080/03601277.2017.1386406

A new research agenda: instructional practices of activists mobilizing for science

Meghnaa Tallapragada

ABSTRACT
Recently, many scientists and science advocates have taken the responsibility to mobilize for the sake of science. With fake news or "alternative facts" on the rise, many scientists and science supporters are determined to protect the credibility of science and promote evidence-based policy-making. At the core of these mobilization efforts is teaching: making science accessible to the public and policy makers in ways that mitigate false information. This paper argues that communication scholars can contribute to this important conversation through exploring instructional aspects of science activism. The paper proposes potential areas of investigation focused on intersections among science, mobilization, teaching, and learning. To do so, such research will involve scientists and nonscientists, as well as lifelong and first-time activists, in negotiating instructional practices to mobilize for science.

Appalled by the growing era of post-truths and alternative facts, there has been a surge in activism by scientists and science advocates calling for measures to ensure the credibility and use of accurate scientific information in policy-making (March for Science, n.d.; Vernon, 2017). The inaugural *March for Science* on April 22, 2017 and the subsequent *March for Science* on April 14, 2018 had many scientists and science supporters—lifelong and first-time activists—take to the streets to advocate for science, urging the current Trump administration to implement evidence-based policies and demonstrating the importance of credible scientific information among lay publics and politicians (March for Science, n.d; Myers, Kotcher, Cook, Beall, & Maibach, 2018). Many scientists who never marched before (and who are typically encouraged not to get political) mobilized for the sake of science (Kotcher, Myers, Vraga, Stenhouse, & Maibach, 2017; Myers et al., 2018; Nelson & Vucetich, 2009). With the steep growth in activism for science, this article proposes a new research agenda investigating the instructional practices involved with science activists and the lay public.

Activism and mobilization are in part, by their nature, instructional processes. Activists learn about an issue themselves and then strive to frame their learned grievances about that issue strategically to align the goals and ideology of the movement with the beliefs and values of individuals in the communities being targeted for mobilization (Snow, Benford, McCammon, Hewitt, & Fitzgerald, 2014; Snow, Rochford, Worden, & Benford, 1986). Community members often learn about the issue from activists, get engaged with those activists, and then (once mobilized) take on the role of teachers to help others mobilize (Snow, Benford et al., 2014; Snow, Rochford et al., 1986). The iterative teaching–learning cycle is at the core of mobilization and, hence, merits investigation by a wide range of communication scholars.

Areas of investigation: communication, teaching, learning, and science activism

Historically, scientific information has been guarded heavily with limited access, given only to the educated, and, if made publicly available, often still couched in technical language only comprehensible to fellow scientists (Gieryn, 1983; Turney, 2008). The fact that scientific information was not readily available to all made educating the public—both formally and informally—problematic (Turney, 2008). That said, the lack of access has rarely kept activists from becoming knowledgeable about scientific issues (see Brown, 1993; Epstein, 1996; Ottinger, 2013) and efforts are continuously being made to increase access to scientific information for nonscientists (Bucchi & Trench, 2008). The struggle lately, though, has not necessarily been about accessibility, but rather about availability. With more scientific information available to both lay publics and policy makers, we must consider the subsequent responsibilities involved with educating multiple constituents about scientific issues. In this paper, four potential areas of investigation are outlined to address these growing instructional issues: the credibility of scientific information; the relationship between learning, literacy, and attitudes toward science; the compliance gaining strategies adopted by activists to stimulate mobilization; and the credibility of scientists and science during the current moment.

First, in a time when many suggest fake news and alternative facts are flooding media (Ferber, 2018; Vernon, 2017), any effective scientific activism must be grounded in credible information. In many of today's activist movements, scientists who are trained in critical analysis of evidence are working alongside lay individuals who are likely only tangentially trained in critical analysis of evidence. Research could fruitfully explore how the meaning of scientific information is negotiated by experts (scientists) and lay publics (novices), including what criteria each group uses to evaluate information and source credibility. Researchers could also study how scientists teach soon-to-be mobilized individuals to critically assess and use scientific information. For example, investigations could include how activists are interacting in an instructional manner to cocreate criteria of credibility; targeting dispositions of lay individuals to stimulate critical thinking; and enacting metacognitive approaches to help individuals stay aware of their learnings, biases, and overall literacy (Halpern, 1998; Mortimer & Scott, 2003). Learning to be critical of evidence is also increasingly important within the communication classrooms that potentially train these current and future activists and scientists; teaching others to "acquire, use, and evaluate information is a staple of communication education [that] communication educators have not sufficiently discussed" (Meyer et al., 2008, p. 31). Starting with research initiated outside traditional classrooms could prove beneficial and feed back into the classroom by providing an understanding of how individuals experience information sources, assess those sources, and teach others to do the same—improving information literacy for themselves and those around them (McGeough & Rudick, 2018).

Another line of investigation could examine the influence of mobilization on science literacy and attitudes toward science. When advocates mobilize for science, how does that mobilization influence participants' practical science literacy (defined as understanding of scientific issues); civic science literacy (defined as developing the vocabulary and motivation necessary to participate in scientific discussions); and cultural science literacy (defined as gaining an appreciation for all things science and developing intolerance for pseudoscience) (Shen, 1975)? There is conflicting evidence about the ways in which science literacy influences attitudes toward science. Some research suggests that knowledge has little to no bearing on attitudes toward scientific issues (Ho, Brossard, & Scheufele, 2008). Other research presents positive correlations between knowledge and attitudes toward science (Allum, Sturgis, Tabourazi, & Brunton-Smith, 2008), and yet other scholars argue that knowing more science can result in affirming one's already held position on science (Drummond & Fischhoff, 2017). To better understand the relationship between literacy and attitudes toward scientific issues, future investigations could explore the processes of knowledge acquisition, placing communication and instruction scholars in a prime position to make important contributions.

For example, researchers could study how—during mobilization—scientists and nonscientists learn by connecting scientific concepts to everyday experiences, to other scientific concepts, and to real world phenomena (Mortimer & Scott, 2003). Scholars could also study whether activists, like many organizational teams, adopt a divide and conquer strategy (e.g., where scientists take the responsibility for understanding the scientific aspects of the issue and nonscientists strategize a communication plan for the activist movement; Lewis, 2004; Wegner, Giuliano, & Hertel, 1985). Although it is possible this approach might not improve practical science literacy, it could potentially improve the civic and cultural science literacy of those engaged in activism, thereby potentially improving attitudes toward science. Future research could explore this possibility. Additionally, through explorations of the interactions between scientists and nonscientists working in more of a collaborative (and less of a divide and conquer) manner, scholars could learn how to increase science literacy on practical, civic, and cultural levels.

A third line of investigation could involve the ways science activists employ compliance gaining strategies (Kearney & Plax, 1992; Snow et al., 2014) to mobilize others to their cause. Scholars could explore the similarities and differences between compliance gaining strategies adopted by scientists and nonscientists and by first-time and lifelong activists. Exploring compliance gaining strategies could also reveal the extent to which activist scientists and nonscientists use top-down approaches (deficit) or bottom-up approaches (dialogue), or both approaches to gain compliance with each other and policy makers as they are teaching their relative audiences about scientific issues (Brossard & Lewenstein, 2010). Researchers could also explore how compliance evolves during mobilization (Roach, 1994); how some resist compliance gaining strategies of the activists (Burroughs, 2007; Kearney, Plax, & McPherson, 2006); and how positive rapport (Lowman, 1984) and socialization (Kearney & Plax, 1992) play a role in compliance gaining between those who are mobilizing and those who are being mobilized, between the first-time and the lifelong activists, and between scientists and nonscientists. All these lines of research could reveal worthy additions to the strategies employed by formal instructors especially for adult learners.

Finally, it is not only important to explore the credibility of information in science activism, but it could also be beneficial to explore ways in which activists gain, enact, and negotiate credibility themselves. Whereas scholars have explored instructor/teacher credibility (e.g., Infante, 1985; Thweatt & McCroskey, 1998), such explorations might be enhanced with research outside the traditional classroom. Scholars could explore, for example, the ways in which the public attributes credibility to scientific mobilizers and activists. This is especially important given that the credibility of scientists and science has come under intense scrutiny in recent years (Kotcher et al., 2017; Vernon, 2017). In particular, there has been some debate over whether or not scientists should take firmer stances on political issues affecting science. While some studies perceive that the credibility of scientists decreases with a firmer stance (Nelson & Vucetich, 2009), others have shown that credibility of scientists does not suffer when they take a firm stance on issues that are politically charged (Kotcher et al., 2017). There is also debate on the role of perceived political ideology on credibility and mobilization efforts. Activist scientists could be perceived as anti-Trump, anti-Republican, or anticonservative, which could politically polarize science and hurt the credibility of science and scientists among Republicans and conservatives (Resnick, 2017; Wessel, 2017).

Since communication scholars have already identified important constructs that influence credibility—disclosing personal information (Johnson, 2011; Mazer, Murphy, & Simonds, 2009), using technology (Schrodt & Turman, 2005), and verbal and nonverbal immediacy behaviors (Teven & Hanson, 2004)—the question becomes, do these constructs also apply outside traditional classrooms to mobilizers and activists (who are essentially teachers in many ways)? Which of these constructs transfer to this advocacy context? What nuances do we have to consider with the mobilizer/activist-as-teacher? What new constructs emerge as influencing the credibility of science, the science activist, and the learning of activist information?

Conclusions

Research on communication and science has often been thought to be the domain of scholars in science communication or science and technology studies; questions of activism have been addressed primarily by social movement scholarship. This article, however, argues that a huge aspect of the contemporary and growing science activist movement involves teaching and learning, making the proposed agenda well suited for scholars invested in communication and instruction. Instructional scholars already acknowledge the importance of communication activism pedagogy (Frey & Palmer, 2014). There are additional opportunities to explore the players in this pedagogy: the mobilizers and activists themselves as teachers and learners and the public who participate in these activist events. The distinct instructional aspects of scientific activism—involving scientists, nonscientists, new activists, and veteran activists all coming together to support scientific causes—offers scholars opportunities to make meaningful, relevant, and timely contributions to conversations about the role and power of communication and instruction in scientific mobilization and activism.

References

Allum, N., Sturgis, P., Tabourazi, D., & Brunton-Smith, I. (2008). Science knowledge and attitudes across cultures: A meta-analysis. *Public Understanding of Science*, *17*(1), 35–54.

Brossard, D., & Lewenstein, B. (2010). A critical appraisal of models of public understanding of science: Using practice to inform theory. In L. Kahlor & P. Stout (Eds.), *Understanding and communicating science: New agendas in communication* (pp. 11–39). New York, NY: Routledge.

Brown, P. (1993). When the public knows better: Popular epidemiology challenges the system. *Environment, 35*, 16–41. https://doi.org/10.1080/00139157.1993.9929114

Bucchi, M., & Trench, B. (2008). *Handbook for public communication of science and technology*. New York, NY: Routledge.

Burroughs, N. F. (2007). A reinvestigation of the relationship of teacher nonverbal immediacy and student compliance-resistance with learning. *Communication Education, 56*, 453–475.

Drummond, C., & Fischhoff, B. (2017). Individuals with greater science literacy and education have more polarized beliefs on controversial science topics. In *Proceedings of the National Academy of Sciences of the United States of America*. https://doi.org/10.1073/pnas.1704882114

Epstein, S. (1996). *Impure science: AIDS, activism, and the politics of knowledge*. Berkeley, CA: University of California Press.

Ferber, D. (2018). Fighting back against "alternative facts": Experts share their secrets. *Science*. Retrieved from http://www.sciencemag.org

Frey, L. R., & Palmer, D. L. (2014). *Teaching communication activism: Communication education for social justice*. New York, NY: Hampton Press.

Gieryn, T. (1983). Boundary-work and the demarcation of science from non-science: Strains and interests in professional ideologies of scientists. *American Sociological Review, 48*(6), 781–795. doi:10.2307/2095325

Halpern, D. F. (1998). Teaching critical thinking for transfer across domains: Disposition, skills, structure training, and metacognitive monitoring.. *American Psychologist, 53*, 449–455.

Ho, S. S., Brossard, D., & Scheufele, D. A. (2008). Effects of value predispositions, mass media use, and knowledge on public attitudes toward embryonic stem cell research. *International Journal of Public Opinion Research, 20*(2), 171–192.

Infante, D. A. (1985). Inducing women to be more argumentative: Source credibility effects. *Journal of Applied Communication Research, 13*, 33–44.

Johnson, K. A. (2011). The effect of twitter posts on students' perceptions of instructor credibility. *Learning, Media and Technology, 36*, 21–38. doi:10.1080/174398842010534798

Kearney, P., & Plax, T. G. (1992). Student resistance to control. In V. P. Richmond & J. C. McCroskey (Eds.), *Power in the classroom: Communication, control, and concern* (pp. 85–100). Hillsdale, NJ: Lawrence Erlbaum Associates, Inc.

Kearney, P., Plax, T. G., & McPherson, M. B. (2006). Student resistance. In T. P. Mottet, V. P. Richmond, & J. C. McCroskey (Eds.), *Instructional communication: Rhetorical and relational perspectives* (pp. 235–252). Boston, MA: Allyn & Bacon.

Kotcher, J. E., Myers, T. A., Vraga, E. K., Stenhouse, N., & Maibach, E. W. (2017). Does engagement in advocacy hurt the credibility of scientists? Results from a randomized national survey experiment. *Environmental Communication, 11*, 415–429.

Lewis, K. (2004). Knowledge and performance in knowledge-worker teams: A longitudinal study of transactive memory systems. *Management Science, 50*, 1519–1533. doi:10.1287/mnsc/1040.0257

Lowman, J. (1984). *Mastering the techniques of teaching*. San Francisco, CA: Jossey-Bass Publishers.

March for Science. (n.d.). Our Mission. Retrieved from https://www.marchforscience.com

Mazer, J., Murphy, R. E., & Simonds, C. J. (2009). The effects of teacher self-disclosure via *facebook* on teacher credibility. *Learning, Media and Technology, 34*, 175–183. doi:10.1080/17439880902923655

McGeough, R., & Rudick, C. K. (2018). "It was at the library; therefore it must be credible": Mapping patterns of undergraduate heuristic decision-making. *Communication Education, 67*, 165–184. doi:10.1080/03634523.2017.1409899

Meyer, K. R., Hunt, S. K., Hooper, M., Thakkar, K. V., Tsoubakopoulos, V., & Van Hoose, K. J. (2008). Assessing information literacy instruction in the basic communication course. *Communication Teacher, 22*, 22–34.

Mortimer, E. F., & Scott, P. H. (2003). *Meaning-making in secondary science classrooms*. Buckingham, UK: Open University Press.

Myers, T. A., Kotcher, J. E., Cook, J., Beall, L., & Maibach, E. W. (2018). *March for science 2017: A survey of participants and followers*. Center for Climate Change Communication: George Mason University. Retrieved from https://www.climatechangecommunication.org/wp-content/uploads/2018/04/March_for_Science_2017_survey.pdf

Nelson, M. P., & Vucetich, J. A. (2009). On advocacy by environmental scientists: What, whether, why, and how. *Conservation Biology, 23*, 1090–1101. doi:10.1111/j.1523-1739.2009.01250

Ottinger, G. (2013). *Refining expertise: How responsible engineers subvert environmental justice challenges*. New York, NY: New York University Press.

Resnick, B. (2017). Scientists are going to march on Washington. Here's why that's awkward. *Vox*. Retrieved from https://www.vox.com

Roach, D. K. (1994). Temporal patterns and effects of perceived instructor compliance-gaining use. *Communication Education, 43*, 236–245.

Schrodt, P., & Turman, P. D. (2005). The impact of instructional technology use, course design, and sex differences on students' initial perceptions of instructor credibility. *Communication Quarterly, 53*, 177–196. doi:10.1080/01463370500090399

Shen, B. S. P. (1975). Science literacy and the public understanding of science. In S. B. Day (Ed.), *Communication of scientific information* (pp. 44–52). Basel: Karger.

Snow, D., Benford, R., McCammon, H., Hewitt, L., & Fitzgerald, S. (2014). The emergence, development, and future of the framing perspective: 25+ years since 'frame alignment'. *Mobilization: An International Quarterly, 19*, 489–512.

Snow, D., Rochford, B., Worden, S., & Benford, R. (1986). Frame alignment processes, micromobilization, and movement participation. *American Sociological Review, 51*(4), 464–481.

Teven, J. J., & Hanson, T. L. (2004). The impact of teacher immediacy and perceived caring on teacher competence and trustworthiness. *Communication Quarterly, 52*, 39–53.

Thweatt, K. S., & McCroskey, J. C. (1998). The impact of teacher immediacy and misbehaviors on teacher credibility. *Communication Education, 47*, 348–358.

Turney, J. (2008). Popular science books. In M. Bucchi & B. Trench (Eds.), *Handbook for public communication of science and technology* (pp. 5–14). New York, NY: Routledge.

Vernon, J. L. (2017). Science in the post-truth era. *American Scientist*. Retrieved from https://www.americanscientist.org

Wegner, D. M., Giuliano, T., & Hertel, P. (1985). Cognitive interdependence in close relationships. In W. J. Ickes (Ed.), *Compatible and incompatible relationships* (pp. 253–276). New York, NY: Springer-Verlag.

Wessel, L. (2017). The marches for science, on one global interactive map. *Science*. Retrieved from http://www.sciencemag.org

I, teacher: using artificial intelligence (AI) and social robots in communication and instruction

Chad Edwards, Autumn Edwards, Patric R. Spence and Xialing Lin

ABSTRACT
Human–machine communication has emerged as a new relational context of education and should become a priority for instructional scholarship in the coming years. With artificial intelligence and robots offering personalized instruction, teachers' roles may shift toward overseers who design and select machine-led instruction, monitor student progress, and provide support. In this essay, we argue that bringing the sensibilities of instructional researchers to bear on these issues involving machine agents, within and outside the traditional classroom walls, is vitally important.

Reportedly, by the end of 2018, Japan will boast a robot news anchor named Erica, a highly human-like android designed by Hiroshi Ishiguro to resemble a 23-year-old woman (Tumboken, 2018). Because Erica can capably recite scripted news writing, ably converse with humans, and project charisma, Ishiguro and others believe she is well suited to a public information-sharing role. However, questions emerge regarding what is gained and lost when the communication traditionally occurring between human beings starts to involve machine partners. Will off-loading repetitive information-labor tasks to robots and artificial intelligence (AI) free humans to pursue more interpretive, creative, and high-value work associated with consciousness? Will people find the experience of receiving information and instruction from machine agents educational, fulfilling, and enjoyable? What are the social and ethical implications for replacing or offsetting human labor with machine agents? Which aspects of design, as well as which contexts of adoption and use, will enhance or diminish our shared values and desired outcomes for the process of communication? And, at the most basic level, to what extent is it even possible for humans and machines to communicate with (and thereby educate) one another?

Already, AI software and embodied social robots are being employed as teachers' aids, tutors, and peer learning specialists in classrooms around the world (e.g., Vasagar, 2017). Forecasts vary, with some educational specialists predicting machine agents will begin replacing teachers in classrooms within the next 10 years as part of "a revolution in one-to-one learning" facilitated by intelligent machines' ability to adapt methods of communication to individual pupils' baseline levels of knowledge and their unique learning styles (Bodkin, 2017, para 1). With AI and robots offering personalized instruction, teachers' roles may shift toward overseers who design and select machine-led instruction, monitor student progress, and provide pastoral support.

Although there is a long history of using machines as educational tools, the introduction of machines that serve as the communication source or interaction partner is both a recent and rapidly developing reality. Human–machine communication (HMC) has emerged as a new relational context of education and should become a priority context for instructional scholarship in the coming years (Edwards & Edwards, 2017). Because HMC has the potential to disrupt some of our most basic assumptions and expectations about communication and education (e.g., that these processes necessarily occur between human actors) and to alter existing educational arrangements and outcomes dramatically, it is vitally important to bring the comprehensive sensibilities of scholars who study communication, teaching, and learning to bear on these issues at the earliest possible stages in design, policy-making, implementation, and evaluation. In the following sections, we discuss how communication can be scripted in the HMC instructional context and then highlight several ways that researchers could use existing teacher/learning variables to start exploring machine agents (AI and social robots) in the classroom.

Human-to-human interaction script for communication, instruction, and HMC

Much of communication is a scripted endeavor (Kellerman, 1992) and this can allow for machine agents to take a more significant role in the educational process as co-instructors. Machine agent teachers use Spoken Dialogue Systems (SDS), or more generally, scripted responses that can instruct and teach. SDS can be defined as "computer systems that use spoken language to interact with users to accomplish a task" (McTear, 2002, p. 91). SDS is used with both AI software (e.g., chatbots) and embodied social robots and aims to imitate human dialogue in a scripted process. The effectiveness of SDS can be rated on how "human-like" the interaction is perceived to be (Boyce, 2000, p. 29). The interpersonal impressions and perceptions of SDS will be a central focus of assessing the use of AI and social robots in an instructional context.

Consequently, it is important to understand how the characteristics and assumptions of human-to-human interactions are played out in HMC. Research demonstrates that people operate on the basis of a human-to-human interaction script when interacting with machine communicators. Generally, people expect their communication partners to be other humans and face greater uncertainty, and lower anticipated social presence and liking, when their partner is instead a machine (Edwards, Edwards, Spence, & Westerman, 2016; Spence, Westerman, Edwards, & Edwards, 2014). One aspect of this human-to-human interaction script is that communication is a heavily scripted process in which priming and prior experience play key roles in the process of selecting and modifying appropriate scripts for use in a given context. Identifying such scripts in an education setting can help to determine best practices for the design of machine agents that teach humans. For example, one common education script involves critiquing and coaching a student on the writing process. A machine agent could do much of this work with the proper scripting. Designing machine scripts would also afford scholars the ability to examine commonly used educational scripts for issues of gendered, sexist, or othering language. In other words, we might be able to "challenge sociocultural oppressions" that can occur in teaching (Fassett & Warren, 2007, p. 3). At the same time, there would need to be a greater understanding of what is lost in the teaching context when the human's role is potentially reduced and when human scripts are designed for machine teachers.

A second aspect of the human-to-human interaction script is that people have an anthropocentric expectancy bias for communication. In the instructional context, people assume teachers will be other humans and may experience positive or negative expectancy violations when an instructor is an AI or social robot. For example, if a student possesses a script for interacting with a human teacher but is told to interact with a social robot as a teacher, increased levels of uncertainty might occur. Levels of uncertainty should decrease after communicating with the machine agent in a learning context, but it is unclear whether human-to-human uncertainty reduction scripts will map to the human-to-robot interaction. Finally, a third aspect of the human-to-human interaction script is that humans nonetheless tend to treat and respond to machine agents as if they were people (Reeves & Nass, 1996). In the classroom, this might lead to both positive and negative outcomes. Does the perceived value of teachers increase or decrease when a classroom comprises both human and machine teachers? Would this change lead to dehumanization of other mentoring-type figures? With these assumptions in mind, many communication and instruction theories, variables, and processes that influence human interaction will likely also be useful for understanding the potential advantages and disadvantages of machine agents in educational contexts both within and beyond traditional classrooms.

Parallels in human–robot interaction (HRI) and instructional communication research

When machine agents play a role in teaching, it is important to consider students' impressions of their source characteristics, message behaviors, and relational skills and capabilities. Each class of factors has been demonstrated in instructional literature to contribute greatly to educational outcomes including learning, motivation, and affect toward teachers and material. A number of historic and contemporary communication variables (e.g., credibility, attraction, immediacy, humor) are already receiving attention in the HRI field, although they typically are addressed with different nomenclature and measurement techniques. As communication researchers, we have the vital opportunity to put our long-standing efforts to study the rhetorical, critical-cultural, and relational aspects of teaching/learning (linked to outcomes of varying desirability) into conversation with the efforts occurring in the HRI field. Ultimately, trans-/multidisciplinary engagement will benefit the effort to understand the implications of replacing/displacing humans in the instructional context and identifying best practices for employing human–machine configurations in the educational space. In the following sections, we sketch some areas of promising overlap in the research agendas of communication, instruction, and HRI fields.

Immediacy

The concept of immediacy, or psychological closeness, has been the focus of many studies (e.g., Allen, Witt, & Wheeless, 2006; Andersen, 1979; Gorham, 1988). Instructor immediacy has been linked to student affective learning (Witt, Wheeless, & Allen, 2004) and to instructor credibility (Schrodt & Witt, 2006). Importantly, instructional researchers have adopted a behavior-centered approach to the study of immediacy, focusing on students' perceptions of the frequency with which instructors display verbal and nonverbal closeness/approach-inducing cues (e.g., inclusive pronouns, smiling, nodding). In the fields of HMC and HRI, the related concept of social presence, conceptualized and referred to by scholars as a feeling that one's partner is real and close (referred to as a sense of *mediated immediacy*; Short, Williams, & Christie, 1976), has been identified as an important perceptual variable for understanding human–machine interactions. Instructional researchers are particularly well suited to examine how specific behaviors, whether performed by a person or a machine instructor, may either result in feelings of connectedness and the associated positive outcomes or produce negative emotions in the classroom environment. As AI and social robots are both in the classroom and increasingly at home acting as tutors (Han, Jo, Park, & Kim, 2005), the study of immediacy with machines is warranted.

Credibility

Whether an instructor is perceived as credible or not is an important consideration in the classroom. Credibility—comprising competence, goodwill, and trustworthiness—has been related to positive instructor and student behaviors in the classroom (McCroskey & Teven, 1999; Schrodt & Witt, 2006). Perceptions of AI and social robots as teaching partners will most likely rely heavily on student impressions of credibility. Edwards, Edwards, Spence, Harris, and Gambino (2016) demonstrated in an experiment that a social robot could be perceived as credible in a college classroom, albeit in a limited role of short-term lecturer. This finding makes sense given what we know of the machine heuristic: the idea that that people often prescribe credibility to a machine because it is viewed as unbiased or free from error (Sundar, 2008).

In the field of HRI, credibility is sometimes referred to as *trust* or *machine trust* (Sanders, Oleson, Billings, Chen, & Hancock, 2011). Manipulating various agent characteristics (e.g., levels of interactivity, social presence, and message behaviors) is a good first step in determining how students will perceive the levels of credibility of their machine instructors. The machine heuristic (Sundar, 2008) is a powerful part of this process. In fact, research suggests that even if the machine agent makes some mistakes, those mistakes might not be enough to reduce trust (Salem, Lakatos, Amirabdollahian, & Dautenhahn, 2015). Factor into these complexities the issues of power and privilege that characterize human-to-human interactions, and there is even more to explore. What role does power and privilege play in terms of establishing and negotiating machine trust? Do machine agents change teacher–student power dynamics (as discussed by Golsan & Rudick, 2018)? Can machine agents avoid giving dominant voices more credibility because of status markers like race or gender? And how do these issues emerge in nontraditional instructional contexts like journalism, where social robots, such as Erica the journalist, will teach and inform audiences about issues of the day? These interactions will occur in a wide variety of contexts outside of the classroom (e.g., journalistic, organizational, and family contexts), hence the study of machine credibility will become important to examine.

Teacher clarity

For students to learn, teachers must demonstrate some degree of clarity in communicating information. Teacher clarity is defined as being "concerned with the fidelity of instructional messages" through the use of instructor behaviors (Powell & Harville, 1990, p. 372) and has a strong relationship with learning (Titsworth, Mazer, Goodboy, Bolkan, & Myers, 2015). Instructor vocalic cues, for instance, are an important part of being clear. With SDS, machine agents can have unique voices, pitches, and accents which may offer distinct advantages (or disadvantages) compared with human instructors with a few clicks of a button. Higher pitched social robots have been rated as more attractive (Niculescu, van Dijk, Nijholt, Li, & See, 2013) and the use of less than robotic voices with more local accents has positively impacted user perceptions (Tamagawa, Watson, Kuo, MacDonald, & Broadbent, 2011).

While altering a human instructor's voice for clarity is practically impossible, this is an instructor behavior that can be changed in HMC (Goble & Edwards, 2018). What role will the perception of a machine agent's SDS have on actual learning, perceived comprehension, and ratings of teacher effectiveness? Does the use of an SDS take anything away from instruction or change how identity shapes the teacher/learner experience? Do issues of technological capabilities make a difference if the AI or social robot is in a small classroom environment or being viewed at home in a tutorial setting? Instructional scholars can address many of these issues being discussed about the nature and quality of SDS voices occurring in HRI with regard to enhancing teacher clarity.

Humor

Humor has long been examined as having a positive impact on the classroom when used appropriately and has been correlated with many positive outcomes (Booth-Butterfield & Wanzer, 2010). The study of humor in HRI is relatively new (Mirnig et al., 2017) but is an important variable to consider (Tay, Low, Ko, & Park, 2016). Based on the limited research, we know that perceived social robot humor has been related to perceived task enjoyment (e.g., task attraction in instructional communication research) by a participant (Niculescu et al., 2013). Additionally, participants give higher likability ratings (a construct similar to social attraction) to social robots that demonstrate perceived positive humorous behaviors (Mirnig et al., 2017). Because humor can be an important part of teaching and learning in a variety of contexts, researchers should examine the ways machine agents can use humor to be effective as co-instructors.

Conceptualization of HMC in the context of communication and instruction

Issues related to communication and instruction can be divided into three categories: learning outcomes, student behaviors and characteristics, and instructor behaviors and characteristics (Mazer & Graham, 2015). In addition to immediacy, credibility, clarity, and humor, many other traditional communication variables can be adapted for use with machine agent instructors using SDS: communication satisfaction (Goodboy, Martin, & Bolkan, 2009), instructional feedback (King, Schrodt, & Weisel, 2009), student engagement (Mazer, 2012), and classroom climate (Myers & Claus, 2012). Also, traditional communication theories—such as speech acts (Searle, 1965) or conversational maxims (Grice, 1975)—might shed light on the crucial interactions between machine teacher and student, both in the traditional classroom and outside in a variety of learning environments. Additionally (and as previously mentioned), critical approaches to communication and instruction may also unveil both positive and negative implications of the use of machine agents in classrooms; deconstructing issues such as access, bias, identity, and displacement of human labor could be important avenues for exploration. In addition to these human factors, scholars could also benefit from examining the unique machine affordances and the impacts of the user interface of machine agents on the teaching and learning setting. Negative attitudes toward robots (Nomura, Suzuki, Kanda, & Kato, 2006) could be a factor in the classroom and might merit exploration as well.

The need to study HMC in instructional contexts will continue to grow as AI and social robot instructors find their way into a variety of teaching and learning contexts—within and outside traditional classroom walls—as co-instructors. HMC can unsettle our basic assumptions and expectations about communication and instruction by adding a new type of teacher, perhaps being perceived more as a threat than an opportunity. Yet scholars invested in communication and instruction have much to add to the conversations about possible design, implementation, and evaluation of these new machine agents in the classroom environment. Much like how Erica, the Japanese robot news anchor, will change how people learn about the news, AI and social robot instructors will change the way people learn our content—within and outside the classroom. While the immediate reaction might be to dismiss this new technology in any instructional context, it is essential for scholars of communication to engage in programmatic and rigorous research that will help guide industry and educators toward best practices.

ORCID

Chad Edwards https://orcid.org/0000-0002-1053-6349
Patric R. Spence http://orcid.org/0000-0002-1793-6871
Xialing Lin http://orcid.org/0000-0002-0474-9743

References

Allen, M., Witt, P. L., & Wheeless, L. R. (2006). The role of teacher immediacy as a motivational factor in student learning: Using meta-analysis to test a causal model. *Communication Education*, *55*, 21–31. doi:10.1080/03634520500343368.
Andersen, J. F. (1979). Teacher immediacy as a predictor of teaching effectiveness. In D. Nimmo (Ed.), *Communication yearbook 3* (pp. 543–599). New Brunswick, NJ: Transaction Books. doi:10.1080/23808985.1979.11923782
Bodkin, H. (2017, September 11). 'Inspirational' robots to begin replacing teachers within 10 years. *The Telegraph*. Retrieved from https://www.telegraph.co.uk

Booth-Butterfield, M., & Wanzer, M. B. (2010). Humor and communication in instructional contexts: Goal-oriented communication. In *The SAGE handbook of communication and instruction* (pp. 221–239). Thousand Oaks, CA: Sage.

Boyce, S. J. (2000). Natural spoken dialogue systems for telephony applications. *Communications of the ACM, 43*(9), 29–34. doi:10.1145/348941.348974

Edwards, A., & Edwards, C. (2017). The machines are coming: Future directions in instructional communication research. *Communication Education, 66,* 487–488. doi:10.1080/03634523.2017.1349915

Edwards, A., Edwards, C., Spence, P. R., Harris, C., & Gambino, A. (2016). Robots in the classroom: Differences in students' perceptions of credibility and learning between "teacher as robot" and "robot as teacher". *Computers in Human Behavior, 65,* 627–634. doi:10.1016/j.chb.2016.06.005

Edwards, C., Edwards, A., Spence, P. R., & Westerman, D. (2016). Initial interaction expectations with robots: Testing the human-to-human interaction script. *Communication Studies, 67,* 227–238. doi:10.1080/10510974.2015.1121899

Fassett, D. L., & Warren, J. T. (2007). *Critical communication pedagogy*. Thousand Oaks, CA: Sage.

Goble, H., & Edwards, C. (2018). A robot that communicates with vocal fillers has ... Uhhh ... greater social presence. *Communication Research Reports, 35,* 256–260. doi:10.1080/08824096.2018.1447454

Golsan, K. B., & Rudick, C. K. (2018). Critical communication pedagogy in/about/through the communication classroom. *Journal of Communication Pedagogy, 1,* 16–19. doi:10.31446/JCP.2018.05

Goodboy, A. K., Martin, M. M., & Bolkan, S. (2009). The development and validation of the student communication satisfaction scale. *Communication Education, 58,* 372–396. doi:10.1080/03634520902755441

Gorham, J. (1988). The relationship between verbal teacher immediacy behaviors and student learning. *Communication Education, 37,* 40–53. doi:10.1080/03634528809378702

Grice, H. P. (1975). Logic and conversation. In P. Cole, & J. Morgan (Eds.), *Syntax and semantics* (pp. 41–58). New York, NY: Academic Press.

Han, J., Jo, M., Park, S., & Kim, S. (2005, August). The educational use of home robots for children. In *Robot and Human Interactive Communication, 2005. ROMAN 2005. IEEE International Workshop on* (pp. 378–383). IEEE. doi:10.1109/ROMAN.2005.1513808

Kellerman, K. L. (1992). Communication: Inherently strategic and primarily automatic. *Communication Monographs, 59,* 288–300. doi:10.1080=03637759209376270

King, P. E., Schrodt, P., & Weisel, J. W. (2009). The instructional feedback orientation scale: Conceptualizing and validating a new measure for assessing perceptions of instructional feedback. *Communication Education, 58,* 235–261. doi:10.1080/03634520802515705

Mazer, J. P. (2012). Development and validation of the student interest and engagement scales. *Communication Methods and Measures, 6,* 99–125. doi:10.1080/19312458.2012.679244

Mazer, J. P., & Graham, E. E. (2015). Measurement in instructional communication research: A decade in review. *Communication Education, 64,* 208–240. doi:10.1080/03634523.2014.1002509

McCroskey, J. C., & Teven, J. J. (1999). Goodwill: A reexamination of the construct and its measurement. *Communication Monographs, 66,* 90–103. doi:10.1080/03637759909376464

McTear, M. F. (2002). Spoken dialogue technology: Enabling the conversational user interface. *ACM Computing Surveys (CSUR), 34,* 90–169. doi:10.1145/505282.505285

Mirnig, N., Stollnberger, G., Miksch, M., Stadler, S., Giuliani, M., & Tscheligi, M. (2017). To err is robot: How humans assess and act toward an erroneous social robot. *Frontiers in Robotics and AI, 4,* 227. doi:10.3389/frobt.2017.00021

Myers, S. A., & Claus, C. J. (2012). The relationship between students' motives to communicate with their instructors and classroom environment. *Communication Quarterly, 60,* 386–402. doi:10.1080/01463373.2012.688672

Niculescu, A., van Dijk, B., Nijholt, A., Li, H., & See, S. L. (2013). Making social robots more attractive: The effects of voice pitch, humor and empathy. *International Journal of Social Robotics, 5,* 171–191. doi:10.1007/s12369-012-0171-x

Nomura, T., Suzuki, T., Kanda, T., & Kato, K. (2006, September). Measurement of anxiety toward robots. In *Robot and Human Interactive Communication, 2006. ROMAN 2006. The 15th IEEE International Symposium on* (pp. 372–377). IEEE. doi:10.1109/ROMAN.2006.314462

Powell, R. G., & Harville, B. (1990). The effects of teacher immediacy and clarity on instructional outcomes: An intercultural assessment. *Communication Education, 39*, 369–379. doi:10.1080/03634529009378816

Reeves, B., & Nass, C. I. (1996). *The media equation: How people treat computers, television, and new media like real people and places.* London: Cambridge University Press.

Salem, M., Lakatos, G., Amirabdollahian, F., & Dautenhahn, K. (2015, March). Would you trust a (faulty) robot?: Effects of error, task type and personality on human-robot cooperation and trust. In *Proceedings of the Tenth Annual ACM/IEEE International Conference on Human-Robot Interaction* (pp. 141–148). ACM. doi:10.1145/2696454.2696497

Sanders, T., Oleson, K. E., Billings, D. R., Chen, J. Y., & Hancock, P. A. (2011, September). A model of human-robot trust: Theoretical model development. In *Proceedings of the human factors and ergonomics society annual meeting* (Vol. 55, No. 1, pp. 1432–1436). Sage CA: Los Angeles, CA: SAGE Publications. doi:10.1177/1071181311551298

Schrodt, P., & Witt, P. L. (2006). Students' attributions of instructor credibility as a function of students' expectations of instructional technology use and nonverbal immediacy. *Communication Education, 55*, 1–20. doi:10.1080/03634520500343335

Searle, J. R. (1965). What is a speech act? In M. Black (Ed.), *Philosophy in America* (pp. 221–239). Ithaca, NY: Cornell University Press.

Short, J. A., Williams, E., & Christie, B. (1976). *The social psychology of telecommunications.* London: Wiley.

Spence, P. R., Westerman, D., Edwards, C., & Edwards, A. (2014). Welcoming our robot overlords: Initial expectations about interaction with a robot. *Communication Research Reports, 31*, 272–280. doi:10.1080/08824096.2014.924337

Sundar, S. S. (2008). The MAIN model: A heuristic approach to understanding technology effects on credibility. In M. J. Metzger, & A. J. Flanagin (Eds.), *Digital media, youth, and credibility* (pp. 73–100). Cambridge, MA: The MIT Press. doi:10.1162/dmal.9780262562324.073

Tamagawa, R., Watson, C. I., Kuo, I. H., MacDonald, B. A., & Broadbent, E. (2011). The effects of synthesized voice accents on user perceptions of robots. *International Journal of Social Robotics, 3*, 253–262. doi:10.1007/s12369-011-0100-4

Tay, B. T., Low, S. C., Ko, K. H., & Park, T. (2016). Types of humor that robots can play. *Computers in Human Behavior, 60*, 19–28. doi:10.1016/j.chb.2016.01.042

Titsworth, S., Mazer, J. P., Goodboy, A. K., Bolkan, S., & Myers, S. A. (2015). Two meta-analyses exploring the relationship between teacher clarity and student learning. *Communication Education, 64*, 385–418. doi:10.1080/03634523.2015.1041998

Tumboken, K. (2018, February 3). Erica the robot destined to be TV news anchor in Japan. *Tech Times.* Retrieved from http://www.techtimes.com

Vasagar, J. (2017, July 13). How robots are teaching Singapore's kids. *Financial Times.* Retrieved from https://www.ft.com

Witt, P. L., Wheeless, L. R., & Allen, M. (2004). A meta-analytical review of the relationship between teacher immediacy and student learning. *Communication Monographs, 71*, 184–207. doi:10.1080/036452042000228054

Bridging campus and community: religion and violence as expansive and socially relevant communication research

Sean M. Horan and Courtney N. Wright

ABSTRACT
Given that instructional communication happens beyond college classrooms, a small group of voices have called for expansive explorations of instructional communication. This essay continues this conversation by calling for research to explore instructional communication's role in religious settings as well as in mitigating violence. Researchers are encouraged to apply instructional communication research to these areas, and enhance the social impact of their research by working in translational formats (e.g., workshops, community partnerships, and popular press writing).

Instructional communication is both "old and new" (Richmond & Frymier, 2010, p. 310) and is "the process by which teachers and students stimulate meanings in the minds of others using verbal and nonverbal messages" (Mottet & Beebe, 2006, p. 5). Given that instructional communication includes "non-traditional instructional settings" (p. 5), we highlight two non-traditional areas that communication researchers are encouraged to apply their knowledge to: religion and violence.

Though no one theory guided our decision to highlight the ideas below, we were driven by a commitment to explore how the communication involved with "teaching and learning" (Mottet & Beebe, 2006, p. 4) can enhance understanding of social issues and mitigate related problems. That said, we are not naïve enough to argue that communication can fix everything. Instead, we believe that systematic study of these issues, utilizing instructional communication research, can partially inform some of these problems. It is in the spirit of Chaffee and Berger (1987) that we make this assertion. They argued that: "The concept of a science of human communication rests upon the optimistic assumption that behavior can be both understood and improved through systematic study" (p. 99). With this in mind, we focus our discussion on two understudied areas of religion and violence.

Religion and violence are cornerstones of human civilization that can have independent and interdependent influences on human development and social interaction. They can also be [mis]perceived as the catalysts of and solutions to various issues plaguing society. Their primacy to social interaction in communities and on campuses are illustrated by their relevance to communication issues surrounding race and citizenship status in present-day America (e.g., killings of unarmed people of color by law enforcement; for one example, see Jacobo & Martin, 2018), debates over sanctuary churches/cities and immigration (Associated Press, 2018), racist speech (e.g., Stone, 2018), mass shootings, and [non]violent protests. Therefore, we situate our research agenda around the utility of instructional communication in understanding and mitigating social issues surrounding religion and violence by (1) considering how external factors permeate communication and instruction, and (2) recognizing the complexity and diversity of individual identities and relational dynamics in instructional settings often overlooked by communication researchers (see Hendrix, Jackson, & Warren, 2003; Hendrix & Wilson, 2014).

Instructional communication's role in understanding religion and religious settings

A handful of communication scholars have examined instructional practices in religious settings. Carrell (2009), for example, explored training religious clergy and associated outcomes. Later, Horan and Raposo (2013, 2015; Horan, Raposo, & Carton, 2014) utilized existing instructional communication findings, such as those pertaining to credibility and misbehaviors, and applied them to the Catholic Church. Extending this perspective, Father Raposo was developing a promising line of research (before his untimely death) that should be built upon. There are several socially relevant problems in religious settings that can be understood via instructional communication. Our first illustration focuses on the Roman Catholic Church. The Roman Catholic Church is a large organization that has problems with church attendance (Saad, 2018), a priest shortage (Breitenstein, 2014), and even church closures (Wang, 2015). Can instructional communication research speak to these issues? Our argument is that it can. As discussed, Horan and Raposo explored priest–parishioner communication, and their collective pattern of findings suggested that there were communication training possibilities for priests that could enhance parishioners' responsiveness and priests' organizational qualities (Horan & Raposo, 2013, 2015). Given that they argued the priest–parishioner relationship is akin to the teacher–student relationship, and that priests engage in many instructional communication practices, continued explorations of this context could better diagnose problematic interactions that might lead to diminished parishioner attendance and/or diminished organizational qualities (which could lead to priests' organizational exit)—both of which contribute to church closures.

Certainly the variety of research findings obtained from instructional communication researchers, including Horan and Raposo's work, could be examined in a variety of religious settings. Therefore, in future studies we encourage researchers to consider differences within, and between, religious denominations, services, activities for religious instruction, and congregation populations and their corresponding needs. What are the instructional communication practices and pastor-congregant relational norms? How do religious leaders use teaching to address the unique needs of diverse congregations? To what extent do social issues permeate the teaching and learning in religious settings—for whom and in what manner? How, and in what ways, is social justice advocacy explicitly communicated in the teaching of certain congregations and absent from others?

Another area of research could involve explorations of communication in multiethnic congregations. Increases in multiethnic congregations in the midst of heightened racial and political tensions has created more dialogue about racial issues across American Protestant denominations and leaders (Shellnut, 2018). However, pastoral leaders of multiracial congregations (of which 71% are white) may lack the skills to manage the social conditions that inhibit social interaction among their congregants (Dougherty & Emerson, 2018). Addressing such skill deficiencies could reduce the increasing exodus of diverse congregants from predominately white churches to African American (Robertson, 2018) and Latino and Spanish-speaking churches instead (Dougherty & Emerson, 2018). Collectively, these challenges also illustrate opportunities for instructional communication research to inform these issues through critical progressive pedagogies (Hendrix et al., 2003) and diversity trainings to enhance interracial/intercultural and intergroup communication.

Finally, researchers would benefit from examining how the topic of religion (faith and spirituality) affects the role of communication in educational settings (e.g., religious studies classrooms, seminaries, and theology programs), as well as the instructional communication approaches of faculty members who teach in private, religious-based colleges and schools. Instructional communication has much to offer to our understanding of specific religious denominations (beyond the Catholic and Protestant illustrations presented here) and the general topic area of religious communication.

Instructional communication's role in understanding violence

It is no secret that violence is an issue in the US (and many other countries). As violence occurs at various levels in rural and urban population centers, it enters into our classrooms. That is, locally, fighting with various levels of escalation occurs in K-12 students and on and/or around college campuses. Tragically, violence can escalate in the form of campus shootings (discussion of guns on campus falls outside the scope of this essay; see Horan & Bryant, 2017). The question becomes, then, what role might instructional communication play in de-escalating situations that can lead to physical violence on campus and in the community?

Instructional communication researchers have long studied verbal aggressiveness and argumentativeness (Myers & Martin, 2006). Research shows that reports of verbal and physical aggression are related (Roberto, Carlyle, & Goodall, 2007), and researchers argue that verbal aggressiveness is partially grounded in the inability to argue (Infante, 1987). Grounded in this argument, Rancer and Avtgis delivered and assessed argumentativeness training to middle school students (Rancer, Avtgis, Kosberg, & Whitecap, 2000). In a related but distinct area of research, Slutkin (e.g., Slutkin, Ransford, & Decker, 2015) argues that violence is a health issue, and through his Cure Violence model (2018) has worked to address violence in Chicago. Instructional communication researchers could, then, combine our understanding of communication, teaching, and learning with Slutkin's research to train individuals to argue better and, potentially, reduce risks for violence. Such research and training would not only expand communication research but also contribute to other disciplines (e.g., psychology and education) as well as aid law enforcement and government agencies in addressing (gun) violence in schools, churches, and public settings.

Naturally, readers may be wondering how they might explore this topic area. We encourage those readers to think about their own understanding of instructional communication and how they might work to be translators in relevant populations. That is, building on the work of Rancer and Avtgis (Rancer et al., 2000), we encourage researchers to design training programs that help individuals develop the skills to mitigate conflict that could become physically aggressive. Such training programs are needed in all levels of education, but also in populations often overlooked by researchers (e.g., individuals who are incarcerated). Scholars should also consider the utility of instructional communication for developing trainings to further enhance the communication effectiveness of populations already skilled in violence protection. As an example, following the events in Ferguson, Dr. Kennaria Brown, a communication scholar, developed a diversity training program for police officers to improve community and police communication (Clevenger, 2018). This program informs police training and offers experience learning to undergraduate students. We encourage others to explore similar partnerships and/or connect with organizations such as Slutkin's Cure Violence (or a local equivalent) to reach populations in need. Researchers wishing to enter this space might also consider pursuit of grant funding that would allow them to support the initiatives they hope to create.

Finally, it is important to study how violence, threats of violence (e.g., bullying), and other aggressive acts (e.g., hate speech) external to the classroom environment might permeate classroom communication and learning outcomes. We offer Work–Life Border Theory (Clark, 2000) as a valuable framework for understanding how students' experiences in their life domain may influence their experiences in their school (work) domain. That is, the theory lays out specific propositions detailing the mutually influential relationships between work and life, and communication researchers have applied it to understanding work–life balance (Hoffman & Cowan, 2008) and workplace romance (Horan & Chory, 2011). Such application of this theory to instructional communication is consistent with previous research applying organizational communication concepts to the classroom [e.g., management style (Chory & McCroskey, 1999), dissent (Goodboy, 2011), upward influence (Wright, 2012)].

We offer two research ideas as illustrations of our reasoning. A student's citizenship status (or that of relatives) is a stressor in the life domain that can spillover into the classroom. Kam, Torres, and Fazio (2017) identified the stressors experienced by high school aged undocumented students, including being bullied. Instructional communication researchers could build on this work, exploring communicative challenges navigated in and around campuses within immigrant populations. Additionally, researchers should consider how under-represented students' communication in class (the work domain) is influenced by distressing experiences in the life domain with racist communication on campus (for example, see Szymczak, 2017) and/or in surrounding communities. Additionally, consider that English et al. (2017) found experiences with police-based discrimination were related to reports of depressive symptoms. Depression is also related to GPA (Hysenbegasi, Haas, & Rowland, 2005), suggesting that race-related incidents can influence learning outcomes. Thus, with great sensitivity, researchers should study current issues that could spillover into the classroom and their implications for instructional communication and learning outcomes.

Concluding thoughts

Based on years of instructional communication research, it is evident that the discipline's dominant focus has been studying communication in traditional college classrooms, with resulting research published primarily in *Communication Education* (see Waldeck & LaBelle, 2016). Departing from this focus, our discussion of religion and violence offers a research agenda diverse in focus and rich with potential to utilize instructional communication to understand and mitigate social problems. The ideas and contexts overviewed reflect broader themes that can guide future socially relevant research beyond the boundaries set by our specific suggestions (i.e., how external factors permeate communication and instruction, the complexity and diversity of individual identities, and relational dynamics in instructional settings). We do note, though, one important element: this essay is written as an invitation for future research, but not offered as an invitation to exploit potentially vulnerable populations who are under-represented in research. Our ideas pertain to areas that are at the core of individuals' identities and, consequently, researchers must be mindful of the delicacy needed in executing this type of research—treating participants as people, honoring their voices and perspectives, and using research to describe and potentially improve the quality of their lives.

That said, we conclude by encouraging researchers to utilize findings in translational formats. By not reaching across campus (Richmond & Frymier, 2010) and/or into local schools and communities, we create opportunities for pseudocommunication experts to offer guidance and training (see Dunbar & Gordon, 2006). Therefore, we suggest instructional communication researchers specifically, and communication researchers generally, work in translational formats via teacher training, workshops, community partnerships, and popular press writing. Our own experiences working in these areas can attest to the benefits of these endeavors for advancing research and visibility of the discipline. Ultimately, this discipline's researchers should be the go-to source for evidence-based recommendations guiding instructional communication practices.

This discipline certainly has value, and wide application—it is the job of future scholars to explore these opportunities fully.

References

Associated Press. (2018, June 28). About 575 people arrested protesting Trump's immigration policy. *Bloomberg*. Retrieved from https://www.bloomberg.com

Breitenstein, D. (2014, May). U.S. Catholics face shortage of priests. Retrieved from https://www.usatoday.com/story/news/2014/05/25/us-catholics-face-shortage-of-priests/9548931/

Carrell, L. (2009). Communication training for clergy: Exploring impact on the transformative quality of sermon communication. *Communication Education*, *58*, 15–34. doi:10.108003634520802235528

Chaffee, S. H., & Berger, C. R. (1987). What communication scientists do. In C. R. Berger & S. H. Chaffee (Eds.), *Handbook of communication science* (pp. 99–122). Newbury Park, CA: Sage.

Chory, R. M., & McCroskey, J. C. (1999). The relationship between teacher management communication style and affective learning. *Communication Quarterly, 47,* 1–11. doi:10.1080/01463379909370120

Clark, S. C. (2000). Work/family border theory: A new theory of work/family balance. *Human Relations, 53,* 747–770. doi:10.1177/0018726700536001

Clevenger, R. (2018, January). Berea College: Diversity training in police departments. *Private University Product and News, 8–12.* Retrieved from http://www.pupnmag.com/article/berea-college-diversity-training-police-departments/

Cure Violence. (2018). Retrieved from http://cureviolence.org

Dougherty, K. D., & Emerson, M. O. (2018). The changing complexion of American congregations. *Journal for the Scientific Study of Religion, 57,* 24–38. doi:10.1111/jssr.12495

Dunbar, N. E., & Gordon, A. (2006). *Popular self-help books on communication in relationships: Who's writing them and what advice are they giving?* Paper presented at the annual meeting of the National Communication Association, San Antonio, TX.

English, D., Bowleg, L., del Rio-Gonzalez, A. M., Tschann, J. M., Agans, R. P., & Malebranche, D. J. (2017). Measuring Black men's police-based discrimination experiences: Development and validation of the police and law enforcement (PLE) scale. *Cultural Diversity and Ethnic Minority Psychology, 23,* 185–199. doi:10.1037/cdp0000137

Goodboy, A. K. (2011). Instructional dissent in the college classroom. *Communication Education, 60,* 296–313. doi:10.1080/03634523.2010.537756

Hendrix, K. G., Jackson, R. L., & Warren, J. R. (2003). Shifting academic landscapes: Exploring co-identities, identity negotiation, and critical progressive pedagogy. *Communication Education, 52,* 177–190. doi:10.1080/0363452032000156181

Hendrix, K. G., & Wilson, C. (2014). Virtual invisibility: Race and communication education. *Communication Education, 63,* 405–428. doi:10.1080/03634523.2014.934852

Hoffman, M. F., & Cowan, R. L. (2008). The meaning of work/life: A corporate ideology of work/life balance. *Communication Quarterly, 56,* 227–246. doi:10.1080/01463370802251053

Horan, S. M., & Bryant, L. E. (2017). Guns on campus: Creating research to inform practice. *Communication Education, 66,* 488–490. doi:10.1080/03634523.2017.1341050

Horan, S. M., & Chory, R. M. (2011). Understanding work-life blending: Credibility implications for those who date at work. *Communication Studies, 62,* 563–580. doi:10.1080/10510974.2011.582663

Horan, S. M., & Raposo, P. (2013). Priest as teacher I: Understanding source credibility. *Journal of Communication and Religion, 36*(1), 73–91.

Horan, S. M., & Raposo, P. (2015). Priest as teacher III: Parishioners' responsiveness and priests' vocational qualities. *Communication Quarterly, 63,* 239–253. doi:10.1080/01463373.2015.1039715

Horan, S. M., Raposo, P., & Carton, S. T. (2014). Priest as teacher II: Understanding priests' communicative misbehaviors. *Communication Quarterly, 62,* 18–35. doi:10.1080/01463373.2013.822902

Hysenbegasi, A., Haas, S. L., & Rowland, C. R. (2005). The impact of depression on the academic productivity of university students. *The Journal of Mental Health Policy and Economics, 8,* 141–151.

Infante, D. A. (1987). Aggressiveness. In J. C. McCroskey & J. A. Daly (Eds.), *Personality and interpersonal communication* (pp. 157–192). Newbury Park, CA: Sage.

Jacobo, J., & Martin, K. (2018, June 27). "We have a battle to fight": Family of unarmed black teen killed by cops wants a conviction, attorney says. *ABC News.* Retrieved from https://abcnews.go.com

Kam, J. A., Torres, D. P., & Fazio, K. S. (2017, November). *Identifying individual and family level coping strategies as sources of resilience and thriving for undocumented youth of Mexican origin.* Paper presentation at the annual meeting of the National Communication Association, Dallas, TX.

Mottet, T. P., & Beebe, S. A. (2006). Foundations of instructional communication. In T. P. Motet, V. P. Richmond, & J. C. McCroskey's (Eds.), *Handbook of instructional communication: Rhetorical and relational perspectives* (pp. 3–32). Boston, MA: Allyn & Bacon.

Myers, S. A., & Martin, M. M. (2006). Understanding the source: Teacher credibility and and aggressive communication traits. In T. P. Motet, V. P. Richmond, & J. C. McCroskey's (Eds.),

Handbook of instructional communication: Rhetorical and relational perspectives (pp. 67–88). Boston, MA: Allyn & Bacon.

Rancer, A. S., Avtgis, T. A., Kosberg, R. L., & Whitecap, V. G. (2000). A longitudinal assessment of trait argumentativeness and verbal aggressiveness between seventh and eighth grades. *Communication Education, 49,* 114–119. doi:10.1080/03634520009379197

Richmond, V. P., & Frymier, A. B. (2010). Communication education and instructional development. In J. W. Chesebro (Ed.), *A century of transformation: Studies in honor of the 100th anniversary of the eastern communication association* (pp. 310–328). New York, NY: Oxford.

Roberto, A. J., Carlyle, K. E., & Goodall, C. E. (2007). Communication and corporal punishment: The relationship between self-report parent verbal and physical aggression. *Communication Research Reports, 24,* 103–111. doi:10.1080/08824090701304741

Robertson, C. (2018, March 9). A quiet exodus: Why Black worshipers are leaving white evangelical churches. *New York Times.* Retrieved from https://www.nytimes.com

Saad, L. (2018, April). Catholics' church attendance resumes downward slide. Retrieved from https://news.gallup.com/poll/232226/church-attendance-among-catholics-resumes-downward-slide.aspx

Shellnut, K. (2018, June 22). Guess who's coming to church: Multiracial congregations triple among protestants. *Christianity Today.* Retrieved from https://www.christianitytoday.com

Slutkin, S., Ransford, C., & Decker, B. R. (2015). Cure violence: Treating violence as a contagious disease. In M. D. Maltz & S. K. Rice (Eds.), *Envisioning criminology: Researchers on research as a process of discovery* (pp. 43–56). New York: Springerlink.

Stone, G. R. (2018, May 30). Roseann Barr and the NFL: What counts as free speech? *Rolling Stone Magazine.* Retrieved from https://www.rollingstone.com

Szymczak, D. (2017, December 19). Racist propaganda is tearing this Texas university apart. *Vice News.* Retrieved from https://news.vice.com

Waldeck, J. H., & LaBelle, S. (2016). Theoretical and methodological approaches to instructional communication. In P. L. Witt (Ed.), *Communication and learning* (pp. 67–101). Berlin: DeGruyter Mouton.

Wang, H. L. (2015). 'It's all about church closings': Catholic parishes shrink in Northeast, Midwest. Retrieved from https://www.npr.org/2015/09/14/436938871/-it-s-all-about-church-closings-catholic-parishes-shrink-in-northeast

Wright, C. N. (2012). Educational orientation and upward influence: An examination of students' conversations about disappointing grades. *Communication Education, 61,* 271–289. doi:10.1080/03634523.2012.671949

Health communication as an instructional communication context beyond the classroom

Teresa L. Thompson

As scholars and practitioners who study and teach communication and education, we are intimately aware of the interrelationships between communication and pedagogy. More importantly, we are cognizant of the fact that education is not confined to the classroom context. The scholarship on communication pedagogy that has been published over the decades in *Communication Education* has made evident the contextual breadth of the educational environment. This special issue continues and expands our appreciation and awareness of this breadth.

As the editor for 30+ years of the journal *Health Communication*, my attention is naturally drawn to the implications of this expansion to communication contexts related to health and health care delivery. The study and practice of health communication have never been confined to the classroom context, as health communication is inherently practice-oriented while being simultaneously based in theory. The Hoffmann-Longtin et al. piece in this issue does an admirable job of reviewing some of the classroom-based pedagogy related to care provider–patient communication skills training while going well beyond that context in the new research reported within the article. The focus on science communication in the Tallapragada piece is also directly related to the health communication context, as most health communication is based on science. Of emerging interest in the area of health communication, however, is the focus evident in the Lee and Will article on fake news and misinformation. Although the term fake news is a relatively recent addition to common vocabulary, with an emphasis on the political, fake news and misinformation as concepts have been studied within health communication for a number of years. In fact, many important health issues have been poorly and inadequately reported in the traditional and social media for some time. Just as fake news has important political implications, it also has life-threatening, bottom-line health consequences. One of the pieces in this special issue mentions a fundamental example of this in the discussion of vaccination issues and the misrepresentation of them in the media. This is a vitally important issue, although it is not the only one that has been examined in depth by health communication researchers.

Although there are numerous examples of fake health news that have been studied in the two flagship health communication journals, *Health Communication* and the *Journal of Health Communication*, space precludes a thorough report of these. The interested reader is referred to Krishna and Thompson (in press) for a more detailed discussion of the relevant work, as this focus on both description and consequences of fake health news/misinformation is one of the exciting and promising directions for instructional communication research that extends beyond the classroom and is worthy of study. Significant issues related to fake health news that have been studied in the two aforementioned journals include: the use of aspirin for heart disease prevention; obesity and diet; nutrition; food advertising; autism (both as it relates to vaccination and apart from that focus); cosmetic surgery; vaccine risk (again, both related and unrelated to autism); human papillomavirus (HPV); teen pregnancy; meat crises (dioxin and "Mad Cow Disease"), Truvada and other pre-exposure prophylaxis meds; HIV/AIDS; sugar/sweeteners; medical tourism; breastfeeding; smoking/e-vaping/waterpipes; a variety of types of cancer; genetic carrier screening; cyberbullying; suicide; Ebola; SARS; Zika; polio; cybercoping; mental health; medical overtreatment; exercise; OTC drugs; DTC drug advertising; diabetes; H1N1; bedbugs; hearing loss; reproductive health; sun protection; toxic risks; steroids; mammography; alternative medicine; Alzheimer's; and natural, man-made, and slow-motion disasters. What research on all of these issues indicates is that the information that is provided in the media about the topics is inadequate and misleading. Some of it is deliberately fake—disinformation—and some is thoughtlessly misinforming through lack of care in the translation of the original research to mediated representations of it.

This focus on fake health news/misinformation is obviously important. It is but one example, however, of a growing and promising area of instructional health communication research that goes well beyond the classroom. Related to this is the work that has been begun by Cline (2003, 2011) on everyday health communication. Rather than focusing exclusively on health communication that occurs between providers and patients in the formal health care context, Cline suggests an expansion of our focus to the information that we as patients all receive from a variety of "everyday" contexts. Building on this work provides important directions on which new researchers are beginning to develop scholarly agendas. Additionally, an examination of current submissions to *Health Communication* indicates that a variety of social media-related topics dominate research interest at the present time. As these media expand, work on the themes and impacts of these also expand. As is evident in several of the articles in this special issue of *CE*, this is not unique to health-related communication work.

Other new and exciting directions for communication work related to health-care are represented by work on male involvement in maternal health, texting prevention, pollution and other environmental issues, hand-washing, and anger or disgust appeals. Those studying instructional communication in health contexts could contribute to this topic, for instance, through exploring gendered learning environments and educational campaigns focused on particular populations. Another expanding focus of research in the area of instructional communication in health contexts is related to mental health. The representation of mental health issues in the media is a part of this, as it is likely to have impacts on the stigmatization of mental health societally and, thus, willingness to seek treatment. It seems prudent to conduct more instructional health communication research focused on debunking some of the myths being perpetuated in social media about mental health. Also related to mental health is research on interactions between mental health professionals and patients and that on communication within couples/families about mental health. Disclosure about mental health is problematic, and work focusing on this is an important and emerging area. Instructional researchers could bring expertise to this area by making explicit the educational implications of their research as we work toward decreasing stigmatization of mental health concerns.

As we continue to look ahead at the intersections between communication and education within the broad instructional context, we may anticipate work developing with foci on suicide representations, end-of-life communication, narratives, visual communication, and crowdfunding as it relates to health issues. Interpretation and multilingual communication are emerging areas of study, reflecting cultural and migration changes. The importance of these issues is likely obvious to *CE* readers, and researchers examining them are and will continue to incorporate an educational focus in their work. The work on suicide representations, for instance, culminates in education for journalists about how to cover suicide in ways that do not lead to copy-cat suicides.

Two additional outcome variables are also in need of examination by health communication researchers and could provide interesting opportunities for collaboration with instructional researchers: adherence to medical treatment and medical malpractice litigation. Although the links between communication and both adherence and litigation are well established, the pathways through which these links operate are in need of further study. Instructional scholars could collaborate with health communication scholars to address these concerns in ways that will result in effective change within provider-patient interaction and, consequently, in achieving desired learning outcomes. As we look ahead toward research needs, then, this author hopes for more focus on these important outcomes as they interrelate with communicative processes.

Obviously, the goal of all health communication research is educational, in that investigation is focused on changing health related behaviors and communication within health care contexts. Thus, teaching and learning are foundational to our work. The emphasis of instructional communication does not occur exclusively within the classroom. There is much promise for collaborative studies focused in a variety of nonclassroom settings in upcoming research related to communication teaching, learning, and health.

References

Cline, R. (2003). Everyday interpersonal communication and health. In T. L. Thompson, A. Dorsey, K. I. Miller, & R. Parrott (Eds.), *Handbook of health communication* (pp. 285–314). Mahwah, NJ: Lawrence Erlbaum Assoc.

Cline, R. (2011). Everyday interpersonal communication and health. In T. L. Thompson, R. Parrott, & J. F. Nussbaum (Eds.), *Routledge handbook of health communication* (2nd ed., pp. 348–368). New York: Routledge/Taylor and Francis.

Krishna, A., & Thompson, T. L. (in press). Health communication and misinformation. *American Behavioral Scientist*.

Response to special issue on communication and instruction beyond the traditional classroom

Matthew W. Seeger

Communication is among the most practical of disciplines and has a rich history. James McCrosky (1984) noted that some of the oldest texts ever discovered provide advice on speaking effectively. A fragment of the Egyptian parchment "The Instruction addressed to Kagemni" (dated between 1929 BC and 1895 BC) provides guidance on communication, virtues, and wisdom. Much of the history of the communication field can be traced to the need to instruct others in the skills of effective communication. The first professional association for the field was the "National Association of the Academic Teachers of Public Speaking" and was established to address the need to teach and promote the oral performance of English (Cohen & Craig, 1995). In fact, one could even argue that instruction is at the very center of the communication disciplines.

The prominence of communication and instruction has diminished, however, as new subfields have emerged and expanded. In some ways, interpersonal, organizational, health, and media (among others) have supplanted communication education as the prominent subfield within our discipline as evidenced by a growing number of scholars being drawn to them. As these subfields emerged and expanded, communication education was pigeon-holed by some as a subfield intended only for speech teachers, especially those teaching the college communication fundamentals courses and those teaching in k12 contexts (e.g., Cohen, 1994; Craig & Carlone, 1998). Increasingly, however, the pigeon seems to be escaping the hole and flying the coop, and, by so doing, illustrating the relevance of communication in instruction to a wide variety of organizational and professional contexts.

This special issue on communication and instruction is part of that larger trend. The six essays published here all seek to extend principles of communication and instruction. They share an instrumental view of communication as a way to address problems and deficiencies and simultaneously positon instructional communication research squarely within larger organizational and professional communication contexts. In addition, they demonstrate the ubiquity and relevance of not only teaching communication principles and skills across contexts beyond traditional classrooms, but also conducting instructional communication research dedicated to informing and improving upon such practices.

The range of contexts represented in these articles is quite broad, from religious organizations in *Context matters (violence training in churches)* to workplaces in *Spewing Nonsense [or not]: Communication competence and socialization in optics and photonics workplaces* to the emerging world of artificial intelligence in *I, Teacher: Using AI and*

Social Robots in Instructional Communication. This suggests that communication skills are essential to almost all social contexts where symbols, messages, and information are exchanged. The means of instructional communication are also quite ubiquitous as demonstrated by the innovative use of applied improvisational theater in *Teaching Advocacy Communication to Pediatric Residents: The Efficacy of Applied Improvisation as a Training Tool.* The essays also demonstrate the diversity of communicative behaviors targeted by instructional communication. The instructional needs addressed are also expansive as described in *Fake news, phishing, and fraud: A call for research on digital media literacy education outside the classroom* to create media literacy, and the effort to instruct scientists in advocacy as illustrated in *A New Research Agenda: Instructional Practices of Activists Mobilizing for Science.*

These essays, then, speak to the continued vitality, diversity, and relevance of instructional communication especially as it is practiced and examined in nontraditional contexts. A wide range of individual, social, professional, organizational, and economical needs are addressed by instructional communication. These communication skills help solve problems, address critical needs, promote resolution of larger public policy issues, and are essential to development and innovation.

With these strengths in mind, however, I believe these essays also speak to some of the limitations to be overcome when applying current concepts of instructional communication in nontraditional contexts. Moreover, I also believe some scholars are beginning to address them in their instructional work beyond the classroom.

First, these essays do not appear to approach instructional communication using a unified and coherent definition. There is confusion, for example, over communication instruction and instructional communication. Teaching advocacy is a form of communication instruction because the target of the instruction is communicative behavior. Violence prevention may or may not involve targeting a communicative behavior. Such instruction, for example, could focus on teaching people gun safety. In almost all cases, instruction requires communicative behaviors, even if the sender is a machine, while not all instruction has improved communication as its goal. Conversely, instructional communication is about the effect of communication *in* instructing. In other words, instructional communication research might focus on designing and testing instructional messages as they lead to desired learning outcomes in a given context (Sellnow & Kaufmann, 2018). Clarifying this distinction is important to creating a research agenda that can produce generalizable insights.

Also important to an effective research agenda is a body of unifying theory. With some notable exceptions such as the IDEA model (Sellnow, Lane, Sellnow, & Littlefield, 2017) and the instructional beliefs model (Weber, Martin, & Myers, 2011), among others, instructional communication research continues to depend heavily on theory from other areas of communication scholarship. While there is value in applying theories developed in other subfields and other disciplines, instructional communication research conclusions ought to focus on how these theories are extended and transformed in ways that make them distinct when applied to instructional research.

Two areas of theorizing could be especially fruitful with regard to instructional research beyond traditional classrooms. First, a theory of instructional needs based on context could help focus the efforts of investigators. Such a theory would seek to explain the conditions that give rise to the need for instructional communication and how instructional communication is a functional and intentional activity that satisfies specific needs or skill deficits. For example, instructional communication in the area of risk and crisis arises from a specific need of individuals, groups, organizations, and communities to protect themselves. Often, this is a very immediate need that differs from the need for public advocacy or professional development in distinct ways.

A second theory of instructional communication that could be extremely useful in a variety of contexts would seek to describe the range of contexts for this form of communication and the associated requirements. Formal communication instruction within organizational contexts, for example, is a well-established area of consulting practice typically associated with organizational communication. Teaching advocacy to members of a profession would represent a different context with unique requirements. Some contexts such as continuing education and professional certification programs are highly structured, while others such as instructional communication for interested community members may be very informal. Understanding the range of contexts and their associated requirements would enhance both research and practice.

A final suggestion for research concerns moving beyond questions about the effectiveness of instructional communication to questions about ethics. Simply stated, are we instructing people in the right things that will serve outcomes that are ethical? Too often, communication skills and techniques have been used to manipulate, deceive, distort, and oppress. The articulation of ethical principles positioned for the use of instructional communication in nontraditional contexts could make one important step toward insuring that what we teach others is used responsibly.

Conclusion

It is hard to overstate the importance of instructional communication as it is applied in nontraditional contexts. The future of the communication field will increasingly rely on demonstrating that it is among the most practical of disciples and that communication can solve problems, address needs, promote resolution of larger public policy issues, and do so in ways that serve ethical goals. Instructional communication and research beyond traditional classrooms certainly ought to be included in the scholarly exchange as it contributes to achieving those goals.

References

Cohen, H. (1994). *The history of speech communication: The emergence of a discipline, 1914–1945.* Washington, DC: National Communication Association.

Cohen, H., & Craig, R. T. (1995). *The history of speech communication: The emergence of a discipline.* Annandale, VA: Speech Communication Association. Pluralism. Disagreement, and the Status of Argument in the Public Sphere, 137.

Craig, R. T., & Carlone, D. A. (1998). Growth and transformation of communication studies in U.S. higher education: Towards a reinterpretation. *Communication Education, 47*(1), 67–81.

McCrosky, J. (1984). Communication competence: The elusive construct. In R. N. Bostrom (Ed.), *Competence in communication: A multidisciplinary approach* (Vol. 66, pp. 259–268). Beverly Hills, CA: SAGE Publications, Incorporated.

Sellnow, D. D., & Kaufmann, R. (2018). Instructional communication and the online learning environment: Then, now, next. In M. L. Houser & A. M. Hosek (Eds.), *Handbook of instructional communication* (pp. 195–206). New York: Routledge.

Sellnow, D. D., Lane, D. R., Sellnow, T. L., & Littlefield, R. S. (2017). The IDEA model as a best practice for effective instructional risk and crisis communication. *Communication Studies, 68*(5), 552–567.

Weber, K., Martin, M. M., & Myers, S. A. (2011). The development and testing of the instructional beliefs model. *Communication Education, 60*(1), 51–74.

A call for a pedagogy of empathy

Carolyn Calloway-Thomas

In May 2018, while traveling in the small, quaint Alpine village of Zermatt, Switzerland, I saw a sweet sign painted on an express train that stopped me in my tracks. It said, "Nothing's sweeter than harmony." Within a nanosecond, however, I was arrested by a subtext at the bottom of the attractive advertisement (in small print!), which proclaimed, "Switzerland's most loved chocolate!" In spite of the unexpected linguistic detour, and in spite of the fact that the sign referred to delectable dark chocolate, the slogan brought unalloyed joy to my heart. I stood still, reflected on what codes are worthy of the humane treatment of others, and hoped for a different kind of existence for humankind, one a huge distance from the following depressing, troubling events.

On Sunday, October 1, 2017, Stephen Paddock, a retired accountant of Mesquite in Nevada, in the United States, fired rounds from his window in Mandalay Bay hotel in Las Vegas, killing 59 people (Locke, 2017). One year ago, Rohingya refugees fleeing Rakhine state in Myanmar (formerly Burma), began a desperate trek into Bangladesh (Oxfam International). As I write this piece, many refugees are still stranded in "no man's land," and are living in makeshift camps in unhygienic conditions. According to a 2016 United Nations Refugee Agency report, "65.6 million people were forcibly displaced worldwide … 75 thousand were children traveling alone or separated" (Edwards, 2016). On Saturday, April 21, 2018, rap music giant Kanye West posted a tweet complimenting Candace Owens, one of President Trump's supporters. West tweeted, "I love the way Candace Owens thinks" ("Kanye West Tweets", 2018). Although West did not explain the specific content of Owen's thinking, his words created hotly contested debates and discussions about what it means to be a freethinking global citizen. And for eight years, the repetitive refrains, "Obama is not a U.S. Citizen," "he is a practicing Muslim," rang out across the land (Cohen, 2011).

Perhaps unsurprisingly, another pretty troubling event occurred after I returned from my intercultural travels. On July 18, 2018, Whoopi Goldberg, a co-host of ABC's *The View,* ordered Fox News host Jeanine Pirro off the show, and according to Pirro, Goldberg used expletives while escorting the former from the premises of the ABC studio in New York City (Feldman, 2018). During the 2016 U.S. presidential campaign, Donald J. Trump employed unflattering characterizers to describe his opponents, from "Little Mark Rubio" to "crooked Hilary"—referring, of course, to Senator Mark Rubio of Florida and Democratic presidential candidate Hilary Rodham Clinton.

As I reflected on the provocative essays in this special issue of *Communication Education*, from calls for expansive and socially relevant research to using social robots in instructional communication, I also gained invaluable insights into the usefulness of the cultural concepts in Yuval Noah Harari's (2015) fascinating *Sapiens: A Brief History of Humankind* for teaching and learning inside and outside the classroom. In discussing the imagined order that we have built for ourselves, Harari argues that we need to understand the difference between "objective, subjective, and inter-subjective" concepts. He writes:

> The subjective is something that exists depending on the consciousness and beliefs of a single individual. It disappears or changes if that particular individual changes his or her beliefs … The inter-subjective is something that exists within the communication network linking the subjective consciousness of many individuals. If a single individual changes his or her beliefs, or even dies, it is of little importance. However, if most individuals in the network die or change their beliefs, the inter-subjective phenomenon will mutate or disappear. Intersubjective phenomena are neither malevolent frauds nor insignificant charades. They exist in a different way from physical phenomena such as radioactivity, but their impact on the world may still be enormous. (p. 117)

The impact of the ossification of discourse in America is enormous, but there is much that instructional and other communication scholars can do to place people in conversation with each other, with huge consequences for civic society. In this short, "look ahead" piece, I argue that a pedagogy of empathy is a meaningful way of interrupting coarse language and generating trust and goodwill among global citizens. Furthermore, I claim that practicing empathy inclines humans toward sociability and can lead to a more peaceful civil society, one that respects all humans, regardless of ethnicity, class, ideology, profession, religion, race, or sexual orientation. By empathy, I mean the "ability imaginatively to enter into and participate in the world of the cultural Other cognitively, affectively, and behaviorally" (Calloway-Thomas, 2010, p. 8).[1] By a pedagogy of empathy, I mean "knowledge and information-based skills that help global citizens respond to and manage intercultural encounters caringly and competently" (Calloway-Thomas, 2010, p. 214). It focuses on skills that students and other citizens need to develop empathy, factors that influence empathetic competence, and approaches to improving empathetic effectiveness. There are many practical uses of empathy, a toolbox, of which the following three are the most crucial ones for deepening intercultural relationships among human beings around the world.

First, empathy sustains civil society robustly by constituting and promoting human dignity. It is a healthy way for citizens to gain habits that should properly serve our collective interests, allowing for sustained human progress. With passion and conviction, we should invest a great deal of research into how empathy can perfect our fractured human existence. But practically speaking, we can begin to imagine a new inter-subjective consciousness by undertaking the construction of templates of empathetic literacy that reach into classrooms, courtrooms, boardrooms, civic associations, beauty parlors, and public squares, and virtually, via Instagram, Facebook, Weibo, Twitter, and other forms of social media.

But how might we do this? I maintain that communication programs at both the high school and the university level should have lessons and units stitched into them that model how citizens are *supposed* to behave in the presence of others, without violating humans' sacred rights, of course. Just by drawing connections between human dignity and behavior, we can help global citizens recognize that in the moral realm of things, respect for dignity is owed to all humans regardless of their standing in the community. "Humanity itself is a dignity," argues Immanuel Kant (1991) in his book, *The Metaphysics of Morals*,

> for a man (person) cannot be used merely as a means by any man ... but must always be used at the same time as an end. We are under obligation to acknowledge in a practical way, the dignity of humanity in every other man. (p. 255)

In our daily interactions with others, we can all participate in shared decision-making about and be mindful of the common good, "the good we share in common." If global citizens are carved up between locals and globalists, idealists and materialists, Democrats and Republicans, town and gown, rural and urban, CEOs and generals, the rich and the poor, and the center and the periphery, surely the trust that binds people together will wither away, and generous civic talk will be difficult to sustain, if at all. This is what the Stoics had in mind when they grappled with a sense of the ecology of human beings. They reached into the "worldly art of grappling with human misery" and focused their attention "on issues of daily and urgent human significance" (Nussbaum, 1994, pp. 3–4). In the process of grappling with "issues of daily and urgent human significance," history tells us that Stoics gave to the world something even more significant, according to Nussbaum (1994), one of the most authoritative scholars on the subject of the Stoics. They gave humankind the gift of "universal respect for the dignity of humanity in each and every person regardless of class, gender, race, and nation—an idea that has ever since been at the heart of all distinguished political thought in the Western tradition" (p. 12).

Although belief in the possibility of cultivating humanity had not yet been codified in the way intercultural scholars view and study it today, the Stoics provide content, methods, and procedures that are central to understanding empathic human behavior. Given that humane action is rarely impervious to behavior that requires careful and responsible everyday sensibilities about what one ought to do, how, with whom, and under what circumstances, Stoics gave ultimate purpose to things that one can do to create a just and humane society. For the purposes of empathetic literacy, the Stoics expressed explicitly a technique of bringing about a happy condition that prepares the human soul for acceptance of the other. Can we as instructors, educators, laypersons, scholars and practitioners organize our thoughts, arguments, discussions, and everyday talk into more affecting modes of civility without denigrating or demonizing the Other?

If such a universal impulse animated us today, would we have among us individuals who utter words such as, "You can smell Trump's supporters when you walk into Walmart?" Would we demonize and diminish people whose values and beliefs are different from our own? Rather, would we use reasoned discourse and thoughtfulness, while simultaneously promoting compassion in the world? Can we use Stoic and other ideals to advocate meaning-making narratives, which are tied to civic virtue that we craft ourselves—together? The calcification of discourses in what is increasingly becoming a divided United States of America has embedded within it a fierce warning of what happens when we rob others of their protective dignity. As Hannah Arendt (1963) so perceptively wrote about the Nazis, "the trouble with Eichmann was precisely that so many were like him, and that many were neither perverted nor sadistic, that they were, and still are, terribly and terrifyingly normal" (p. 276). In the light of uncivil discourse today,

Arendt's proposition should make us shiver and shiver, and shiver at the thought of what happens when we do not assume goodwill—when we do not identify with another's plight, as we seek to live empathetic and peaceful lives. Pedagogy in the twenty-first century must urgently help restore modes of citizenship suitable for such ideals, and one way we can do this is by practicing empathy.

Second, as I hinted previously, goodwill lies at the very core of a pedagogy of empathy. It is made possible when we give people the benefit of the perceptual doubt. This cognitive, affective, and behavioral value orientation assumes that most individuals seek psychological comfort and congeniality. This is empathetic literacy in vigorous practice. Kant (1785) in *The Metaphysics of Morals* reminds us, "The only thing that is good without qualification is the goodwill" (p. 11). What a beautiful idea! What an alluring way to link the subjective consciousness of one individual to the inter-subjective consciousness of others.

Third, like Danielle Allen (2004), I advocate talking to strangers as a way of cultivating global friendships and participating in the shared, inter-subjective imaginaries that we create for ourselves. Talking to strangers can also become a public conveyor of meaning in our lives, as well as a kind way of humanizing the other. Allen (2004) observes,

> The ability to adopt equitable self-interest in one's interactions with strangers is the only mark of a truly democratic citizen, and to employ the techniques of political friendship would be to transform our daily habits and our political culture. Can we devise an education that, rather than teaching citizens not to talk to strangers, instead teaches them how to interact with them self-confidently? (p. 165)

Note

1. I am mindful that empathy has a "dark side," as I suggest in *Empathy in the Global World* (2010) and elsewhere. Paul Bloom (2016) also implies the idea in his work, *Against Empathy*, where he claims "the act of feeling what you think others are feeling – whatever one chooses to call this – is different from being compassionate, from being kind, and most of all, from being good " (p. 4). My conception of empathy is multifaceted, however, and takes into consideration cognitive, affective, and behavioral components, which together urge humans to be discerning in their treatment of others. In a wider sense, I advocate understanding why people behave as they do, with infinite possibilities for shaping a better world.

References

Allen, D. (2004). *Talking to strangers: Anxieties of citizenship since brown v. board of education.* London: The University of Chicago Press.

Arendt, H. (1963). *Eichmann in Jerusalem: A report on the banality of evil.* New York, NY: Viking Press.

Calloway-Thomas, C. (2010). *Empathy in the global world: An intercultural perspective.* Los Angeles, CA: SAGE.

Cohen, M. A. (2011). Tea party affair. Retrieved from https://www.politics.com/story/2011/04/tea-part-affair-could-doom-go-pO52442

Edwards, A. (2016). Forced displacement worldwide at its highest in decades. Retrieved from http://www.unhcr.org/en-us/news/stories/2017/6/59415614/forced-displacement-worldwide

Feldman, K. (2018, July 19). Jeanine Pirro claims Whoopi Goldberg screamed at her backstage. *New York Daily News.*

Harari, Y. N. (2015). *Sapiens: A brief history of humankind.* New York, NY: HarperCollins.

Kant, I. (1991). *The metaphysics of morals* (M. Gregory, Trans.) New York, NY: Cambridge University Press.

Kant, I. (1785). *The metaphysics of morals*. Retrieved from http://www.earlymoderntexts.com/assets/pdfs/kant1785.pdf

Locke, A. (2017). The Las Vegas gunman chose a terrifying vantage point. Retrieved from http://www.businesinsider.com/stephen-paddock-las-vegas-shooting-weapons-vantage-1

Nussbaum, M.C. (1994). *The therapy of desire: Theory and practice in Hellenistic ethics*. Princeton, NJ: Princeton University Press.

Oxfam International. Retrieved from https://ww.oxfam.org/en/emergencies/bangladesh-rohingya-refugee-crisis

West, K. (2018, July 23). Kanye West tweets about Candace Owens. Retrieved from https://hiphopdx.com/news/id.4674/

Riddles, mysteries, and enigmas: communication, teaching, and learning beyond the traditional classroom

Deanna P. Dannels

I have been a teacher my entire adult life. Every full-time job I have ever had has been in a university setting. Every piece of research I have conducted and published, save *one* study, has been conducted within traditional classrooms. Understandable, right? My research has focused on how noncommunication majors work through the challenges of learning communication skills while also learning disciplinary content. I have also studied how new graduate teaching assistants negotiate communication difficulties of the classroom as they learn what it means to be a teacher. Where better to explore these questions than in the classroom? Where better to learn about the intersections between communication, teaching, and learning than in the classrooms within which these processes occur? Where else could I learn about those tricky issues that riddle novice teachers and learners who are trying to navigate through processes outside of their comfort zones?

Where else? Well, let's start here:

Scene 1: Executive leadership workshop; timed teambuilding activity. Participants: Me, Dimitri (CEO of sales company in Greece).

Dimitri:	"Everyone is stressed. We must change the room, Deanna. We'll never finish if we don't change the room."
Me:	"What are you doing, Dimitri? Get off your phone! We have a task to complete."
Dimitri:	"We have work to do, yes. But we need a little music ... " [*Zorba the Greek* music starts playing from phone, all in room stop and look.] "See: everybody is smiling. Now we can work. All we needed was *Zorba the Greek*."

Scene 2: Graduation morning; parking lot of NC State graduation arena. Participants: Me, Margaret (longstanding housekeeper for building).

Margaret:	"How are you doing this beautiful graduation morning, Deanna? Looks like you are all dressed up and ready to go."
Me:	"Well, I'm all dressed up but not so sure I'm ready to go. I am channeling the dean, can you tell? He's out of town ... and I've got to fill in for him on the big stage in front of oh ... almost 10,000 people."
Margaret:	"You'll be fine. But you don't look much like the dean, darlin'. Why don't you just stick with channeling you?"

Scene 3: Text message exchange about birthday plans. Participants: Me, Emma Grace (my 14-year-old daughter and the birthday girl).

Emma Grace:	"Idk what I'm doing for my birthday. Why do you keep asking me? I'm talking with my friends about it. We will figure it out."

Me:	"Babe, I need to get everything planned. That's why I need to know. It doesn't just come together like magic."
Emma Grace:	"Mom, it doesn't always need to be planned down to the minute. We just have to get the right people together and it will be perfect."

Three interactions; none of which happened in a traditional classroom; none of which were with people who would call themselves teachers; all of which left me with important lessons about navigating through communicative processes outside my comfort zone. Where better to learn about the intersections between communication, teaching, and learning than in the classrooms within which these processes occur? Where else could I learn about those tricky issues that riddle novice teachers and learners who are trying to navigate through processes outside of their comfort zones? From Demitri, Margaret, and Emma Grace. In a parking lot, a teambuilding activity, and over a text message exchange. Three interactions; three important lessons. All outside of the traditional classroom.

Teaching and learning happen everywhere, not just in traditional classrooms. The manuscripts in this special issue evidence that. They show us how we, as scholars and teachers, can thoughtfully interrogate teaching and learning with people who are navigating important lessons in workplaces outside of academia, on topics such as religion, artificial intelligence, activism, and digital literacy. They show us there is much to learn from employees who mentor each other into the communication norms of an organization and from healthcare physicians who learn about the necessary communication skills to help patients mitigate online information about medical ailments. Finally, they show us that there is still much to learn, explore, research, and teach, outside the traditional classroom. My challenge to readers is to continue what they have started. Continue looking outside of traditional classrooms for places and people to learn from and teach. Pursue opportunities for scholarly collaboration outside of the comfort zones of the university setting. Engage with conversations in communities and workplaces where teaching and learning is happening and bring your scholarly expertise to bear on those conversations. Pay attention to what we can learn—from casual conversations to scholarly collaborations—and to what we can contribute.

In a 1939 BBC radio broadcast, when trying to predict Russia's actions in World War II, Winston Churchill commented, "It is a riddle wrapped in a mystery inside an enigma" (Churchill, 1939). I'd like to borrow Churchill's quote here as I leave readers with this challenge. Communication, teaching, and learning: riddles wrapped in mysteries inside enigmas. There is much to explore and much to learn. In parking lots and text messages. From teenagers, CEOs, and housekeepers. With physicians, managers and employees, activists, machines, scientists, and older adults. In religious settings, training programs, workplaces, protests, and social media campaigns. Let's step outside of our comfort zones and dig deeper into the riddles, mysteries, and enigmas that face people who are doing the hard work of teaching and learning outside of academia. Let's channel the best of who we are and engage with those who teach and learn everyday, without calling themselves teachers and students. We are the right people to be there; it will be perfect. And important. And fun. Cue up *Zorba the Greek*; we have work to do.

Reference

Churchill, W. (1939, October 1). *The first month of war [Radio Broadcast]*. London: BBC.

Index

Page numbers in **bold** refer to tables and those in *italic* refer to figures.

Accreditation Council for Graduate Medical Education (ACGME) 31, 38
Against Empathy (Paul) 90n1
Allen, Danielle 90
Amazon Mechanical Turk 56
American Academy of Pediatrics (AAP) 39
antivaccination movement 30–1, 34
applied improvisational theater (AIT) 31, 47; Accreditation Council for Graduate Medical Education 31; advocacy communication 44; advocacy communication (self-efficacy) 46; communication instruction 35; communication techniques 43; coordinated management of meaning 33–5; data collection and analysis 41; description 36–7; effective and ineffective communication techniques 44; health advocacy 32–3; health contexts, teaching and learning 46–7; instructional intervention program 31, 45; media and community 42; *New England Journal of Medicine* 31; participants 40–1; pediatric advocacy rotations 38–40; pediatricians 31; physicians 30, 47; research 46; "Teaching advocacy communication to pediatric residents: the efficacy of applied improvisation as a training tool" 2; training programs 48
Arendt, Hannah 89–90
artifcial intelligence (AI) 3; communication and instruction, HMC 69–70; Human–machine communication 66 (*see also* Human–machine communication (HMC)); human–robot interaction (*see* human–robot interaction (HRI)); human-to-human interaction script 66–7; software and embodied social robots 65–6
audience-centeredness 37–9, 44, 45, 47
Avtgis, T. A. 76

Bakker, A. B. 8, 24n1
Beebe, S. A. 1
Berger, C. R. 73
Berk, R. A. 36
Bloom, Paul 90n1

Brasseur, L. 9
Brown, R. F. 32, 35
Bylund, C. L. 35

Carrell, L. 74
Cegala, D. J. 35
Chaffee, S. H. 73
Churchill, Winston 93
civic science literacy 61
clarity 44
Cline, R. 81
Clinton, Hilary Rodham 87
cocreation 44
Cohen's kappa 12
Cole-Kelly, K. 47
Communication Across the Curriculum (CXC) 9
Communication Education 1, 2, 23, 35, 60, 77, 80, 83, 88
communication in the disciplines (CID) 3, 7–9, 21–4
communication skills training (CST) 35, 36, 47, 48
community advocacy 40
companies, optics/photonics 11
Comskil conceptual model 35
Conrad, J. M. 19
content tactics 8
contextual tactics 8
coordinated management of meaning (CMM) 33–5, 45
credibility 3, 4, 59, 60, 62, 67–70, 74
Cronen, V. 33
"crooked Hilary" 87
cross-occupational communication 3, 21–3
cultural science literacy 61
Cure Violence model 75
cybercrimes 3, 52, 53

"Developing Transferable Knowledge and Skills in the 21st Century" 7
digital media 3, 17; avoidance, scams and phishing 56; beyond the traditional classroom 56; crimes 52–3; fake news, scams

and phishing 52; false online news, 2016 U.S. presidential election 52; information and sources 54–5; Internet users 56; media literacy 52; nondigital natives 53–4; outside the traditional classroom 53; privacy and safety concerns 55–6
directed advocacy 33
distilling 34, 39, 43
"Distilling Your Message" 40
Donovan, E. 35, 46
drills 36

Earnest, M. A. 32
Edwards, Autumn 3, 68
Edwards, Chad 3, 68
Egener, B. 47
Empathy in the Global World 90n1
engineers 10, 19–20
English, D. 76
enigmas 89, 92–3
Epstein, R. M. 36

Facebook 52, 53, 88
FactCheck.org 54
fake health news/misinformation 80–1
fake news 3, 52; *see also* digital media; categories 54; 2016 election 53; and misinformation 80; news media 54
familial-like humor 14–15
Fazio, K. S. 76
fluent modality switching 16–18
follow-up survey summary 43, **43**
fraud 3, 52, 53, 55, 88; *see also* digital media

Gambino, A. 68
Goldberg, Whoopi 87
Gonzalez-Roma, V. 8
Guba, E. G. 41

Half Life 39
Harari, Yuval Noah 88
Harris, C. 68
health advocacy: coordinated management of meaning 33–5; definitions 32–3
health communication: *Communication Education* 80; fake health news/misinformation 81; fake news and misinformation 80; health interventions 1; instructional health communication 81–2; interpretation and multilingual communication 82; *Journal of Health Communication* 80–1; research 82
Hilton, M. L. 7
Hobbs, R. 53–4
Hoffmann-Longtin, Krista 2, 80
Horan, S. M. 4, 74
Hubinette, M. 32–4, 37, 39, 46
human–machine communication (HMC) 4, 68; communication and instruction 69–70; human-to-human interaction script 66–7

human–robot interaction (HRI): credibility 68–9; historic and contemporary communication variables 67; humor 69; immediacy 68; teacher clarity 69
humor 67, 69

immediacy 4, 62, 67, 68
individual-based advocacy 42
informal mentoring 18–20
informal mentor–mentee training 19–20
institutionalized tactics 8
instructional communication 1–5, 56, 73, 83–5, 88; health communication 80–2; human–robot interaction (*see* human–robot interaction (HRI)); religion and religious settings 74–5; understanding violence 75–6
"integrated education" 20–1
Ishiguro, Hiroshi 65

Jones, G. R. 8
Journal of Health Communication 80

Kam, J. A. 76
Kant, Immanuel 89, 90
Kaufmann, R. 4
Kedrowicz, A. A. 24
Krishna, A. 80

Lee, Nicole 3
Lenzmeier Broz, S. 35
Lesser, C. S. 36
Levinson, W. 36
Lincoln, Y. S. 41
"Little Mark Rubio" 87

managers, interview protocol 28–9
March for Science 59
Martin, Kelly Norris 3
McCrosky, James 83
media literacy 3, 84; *see also* digital media
mental health 81–2
mentor–mentee relationship 13
The Metaphysics of Morals (Kant) 89, 90
Mirror 38
mobilization 3, 59–62
Mottet, T. P. 1
mysteries 92, 93

"National Association of the Academic Teachers of Public Speaking" 83
New England Journal of Medicine 31
"non-traditional instructional settings" 73
Nussbaum, M. C. 89
NVivo 12

optics/photonics workplaces: CID 7–9, 21–2; and communication 9–10; communication and instruction in STEM 7; competent communication 13–14; data analysis 12–13; data and participants 11–12; efficient

decision-making 14–18; entry-level employee 6–7; NSF-funded study 10; organizational socialization theories 7–8; research 23–4; setting 10–11; socialization 18–21; "spewing nonsense" 24; teaching 22–4; training 24
organization-based advocacy 42

Paddock, Stephen 87
participants: company/research group focus 11, **12**; demographics 11, **11**
patient–provider communication 46
Pearce, W. B. 33
pedagogy of empathy 87–90
Pediatrics Residency Review Committee 32
Pellegrino, J. W. 7
phishing 3, 52–4, 56
Photograph 39
physicians 30–8, 40, 45, 46–8, 93
Pirro, Jeanine 87
practical science literacy 61
pre- and post survey summary, Bonferroni correction 42, **42**
presumed communication competence 18–19
proactive questioning 13–14
professional training and development 1
Protection Motivation Theory (PMT) 55

Rancer, A. S. 76
Raposo, P. 74
religion 4, 73–5, 77
residency 31, 40
riddles 92, 93
robots 3, 65–6, 68–70, 88
Ryan, Will 3

Salanova, M. 8
Sapiens: A Brief History of Humankind (Harari) 88
Satcher, David 31, 32
Schaufeli, W. B. 8, 24n1
Schein, E. H. 8
science communication 3, 62, 80
scientific activism 60, 62
scientific issues: compliance gaining strategies 61; credibility of science and scientists 62; learning, literacy, and attitudes toward science 61; scientific information 60–1

shared advocacy 33
Slutkin, S. 75
socialization 61; *see also* optics/photonics workplaces
social robots 3, 65, 66–70, 84
social tactics 8
sorganizational socialization 7–8
Spence, P. R. 3, 68
"spewing nonsense" 24
Spoken Dialogue Systems (SDS) 66, 69, 70
Spolin, V. 48
STEM industry 9–10, 20–1, 23
supportive housing systems 32

tactful translation 15–16
Tallapragada, Meghnaa 3
Tatum, N. T. 4
Taylor, J. L. 24
teacher clarity 67, 69
technicians 10, 19
Thompson, T. L. 80
Torres, D. P. 76
traditional classroom: executive leadership workshop 92; graduation morning 92; teaching and learning 93; text message exchange 92–3
TranscribeMe 12
Trieber, R. H. 36
Trump, Donald J. 53, 87
2016 United Nations Refugee Agency report 87
2016 U.S. presidential election 52–4

Van Maanen, J. 8
verbal aggressiveness 75
violence 4, 54, 73–7, 83, 84
Vrchota, D. 9

work engagement 8
Work–Life Border Theory 76
workplace 22–3
workshop, AIT drills: distilling your message 39; improvisation for scientists 38–9; media training 39–40; partnering with the community 39–40; on residents' abilities 38; sections 38
Wright, Courtney 4

Zoller, H. M. 32